The H

MW01244512

Self-Management and Leadership Strategies for Success

By Christopher S. Frings, PhD, CSP

Seven steps to overachieving in business and life

AACC Press
2101 L Street, NW, Suite 202
Washington, DC 20037-1526

ISBN 1-890883-00-X

Printed in the USA

*T*o all of the students and audience members who have given me positive feedback and helped me improve myself over the past 25 years. To Professor Harry Pardue, who instilled in me a work ethic that has been going strong since 1962. To Coach Paul "Bear" Bryant, whose words of wisdom have helped me achieve success.

Disclaimer

Every effort has been made to make this book as accurate as possible. However, there may be mistakes in both content and typography. Use this book only as a guide—not as the ultimate source on the subject. It is sold with the understanding that neither the publisher nor the author is engaged in rendering legal or other professional services to the purchaser. If you require legal or other assistance, seek the services of experts who can meet your specific needs.

Your comments or suggestions are welcome. Please address them to the author:

Christopher S. Frings, PhD, CSP
Chris Frings & Associates
633 Winwood Drive
Birmingham, AL 35226-2837
Telephone: 205-823-5044
Fax: 205-823-4283
E-mail: CFrings@compuserve.com

For additional copies or information about bulk discounts, please contact the publisher:

AACC Press
2101 L Street, NW, Suite 202
Washington, D.C. 20037-1526
Telephone: 800-892-1400
In Washington, DC: 202-835-8733
Fax: 202-887-5093
E-mail: info@aacc.org
Internet: www.aacc.org

About the Author

Christopher S. Frings, PhD, CSP, is president of a consulting and speaking company called Chris Frings & Associates, located in Birmingham, AL. A nationally recognized speaker in the areas of time management, goal accomplishment, stress management, and leadership strategies, he works with organizations that want their people to work smarter and with individuals who want to get more done. Also a specialist in change management, he offers customized presentations on problem-solving during times of change. Dr. Frings is often called "the magical speaker," because he mixes cutting-edge information with magic and humor to create exciting programs for his audiences.

Dr. Frings has more than 30 years of senior management experience. Before becoming a full-time consultant and speaker in 1987, he was laboratory director and senior vice-president at a large regional reference medical laboratory for 20 years. Today he is a clinical professor at the University of Alabama at Birmingham and teaches time management at the university's Leadership Institute. He also serves on the editorial advisory board of several trade journals and newsletters. The author of more than 145 articles and several books, he is the author of one of AACC Press' best-selling books, *The Hitchhiker's Guide to Effective Time Management.*

Dr. Frings received a BS from the University of Alabama at Tuscaloosa and a PhD from Purdue University. He earned certification as a clinical laboratory director from the American Board of Bioanalysis and earned the Certified Speaking Professional (CSP) credential from the National Speakers Association. The American Association for Clinical Chemistry has honored Dr. Frings with an outstanding speaker award each of the past 11 years. He received the magician of the year award five times in Alabama.

Contents

Contents, *continued*

Deserving Success

I couldn't wait for success, so I went ahead without it.
—Author Unknown

Success is doing what you want to do well and getting paid well for it.
—Christopher S. Frings

Do you treat yourself as if you are the most important asset you will ever have?

You cannot be an effective manager and leader if you cannot manage your own life effectively. If you're like most people, though, you are under so much day-to-day pressure that you've lost sight of the importance of cultivating your personal management and leadership skills. This book outlines seven steps that are essential to success and presents practical strategies for making each of them a part of your life.

You know that your car runs better after a tune-up. You, too, can benefit from an occasional management and leadership tune-up. That's where this book comes in. My goal is to give you information you can use to become a better manager right now. This information will help you face a fast-changing workplace in which we are all being asked to do more with less. You'll learn how to change your thinking and your life so that you'll be able to work smarter, not harder, and manage change effectively. You have the ingredients. This book contains the recipe for personal success.

No Deposit, No Return

Back in 1950, many families in my home-town were making do on very little money. My friend Johnny Bob Caradine and I used to gather soft drink bottles and turn them in at the local grocery store for two cents a bottle. One day we had 19 bottles. We figured we had 38 cents coming to us. Back in those days, a Coca-Cola cost five cents and admission to a movie 10 cents. Our 38 cents could buy a loaf of bread and a quart of milk and still leave us with several pennies left over.

But there was a problem. One bottle had "No Deposit, No Return" stamped on it. That meant we received only 36 cents for our efforts. My friend Johnny Bob was kind of slow and just couldn't understand what had happened. I explained that we couldn't get anything back for the bottle, since the person who bought it hadn't paid a deposit. Johnny Bob thought for a while and then asked, "If you don't put anything in, you don't get anything back? Is that right?" I agreed. Johnny Bob's next comment surprised me. "'No Deposit, No Return' is just like life, isn't it? If you don't put anything into it, you don't get much out of it."

Keep this story in mind as you read this book. Making a deposit in terms of your personal education and development is especially important in this era of rapid change and new technologies. Put everything you can into this self-management tune-up, and you'll reap many returns. Although some people might call the rewards luck, you'll know that luck is really opportunity meeting preparation. This book will give you ideas and strategies that will make a difference in your life—if you use them.

The Meaning of Success

Success means different things to different people. What does it mean to you? Power? Close personal relationships? The respect of your peers? Self-satisfaction?

For many people, success means money. But you shouldn't go into a particular field just because it pays well. There is no correlation between money and happiness. Some of the richest people in the world are also the most dissatisfied. If money is your ultimate goal, you will never be able to get enough. And chances are that if you are working only to amass wealth, you won't be happy with what you have to do to get it: the work itself. Satisfaction comes from doing something we enjoy and doing it well.

Success comes before work only in the dictionary. Hard work is the basic building block of every kind of achievement. You can start with an idea or a goal, but before any of your hopes can be realized, you must really deserve your success. Nothing meaningful or lasting comes without working hard at it, whether it's in your personal life or at work.

People who attend my seminars, workshops, and keynote addresses often ask me for advice. Their response to my question "What do you want to do with the rest of your life?" is often "I don't know." That response is a classic sign of an underachiever. These people haven't thought long and hard about what they want. Instead, they want advice that they hope will result in instant success. That simply does not happen. You have to plan for success. You have to first establish the direction you want to head, then travel that road with discipline and perseverance.

The Seven Steps To Success

How do you start on the road to success? With these seven steps.

The seven steps outlined in this book represent a plan of attack. Whether you're striving for success at work or at home, in the classroom or on a sports field, these steps will help you achieve greater results. Because society conditions us to settle for less than our full potential, most of us undersell our abilities. That's why the steps are based on the assumption that we can achieve things we never thought were possible.

Are you an underachiever? You can reach your full potential. But to do so, you have to change your habits. To do that, embrace the seven steps:

1. Put balance in your life with written goals.

2. Create a plan for reaching your goals—and stick to it.

3. Expect the unexpected and become a master of change.

4. Learn from past mistakes and successes.

5. Work smarter by using time management techniques.

6. Control stress.

7. Get better at what you do every day.

And remember that the 10 most powerful two-letter words in the English dictionary are "If it is to be, it is up to me." You are responsible for your own success. But first you must decide whether you are willing to try these ideas. Remember, your success is all up to you.

Before we start exploring the seven steps in more detail, let's look at the characteristics of effective managers and leaders in the next chapter.

• *Chapter One* •

Managing and Leading for Success

The problem with most leaders today is they don't stand for anything. Leadership implies movement toward something, and convictions provide that direction. If you don't stand for something, you'll fall for anything.

—Don Shula

To be an effective leader, you must realize that the business you are really in is the obstacle identification—and removal—business.

—Peter Drucker

Leadership deals with direction. Management deals with speed, logistics, and coordination in moving in that direction. Managers become leaders when they repeatedly find and implement solutions that balance everyday contradictions, inconsistencies, and dilemmas. The key is understanding and influencing the critical variables in a work setting: strategy, employee motivation, core operating competencies, and a leader-based microculture. You manage things, but you lead people!

Ethics

The American Society for Quality Control surveyed corporate managers and reported[1] these findings:

• Most managers believe that they face ethical problems.

• Most managers believe that both managers and employees should be more ethical.

---

[1]*Positive Leadership*, Volume 1: Number 1

- Some managers lower their ethical standards to meet the essential requirements of their jobs.

- Managers act more ethically with friends than with strangers.

- Companies can influence business ethics.

Playing by the rules is essential. Effective managers know the rules to ensure that they don't break them inadvertently. The newspapers are full of stories about leaders and managers who have broken the rules, paid huge fines, and even gone to jail. That jeopardizes the entire team's credibility—and future. Coach Paul "Bear" Bryant always told us to "play by the rules." Leaders who are effective for the long haul follow that advice.

Characteristics of Effective Leaders

Are you an effective leader? Here are some of the characteristics to look for:

- Are you a good manager?

- Do you think "outside the box"? "Outside the box" is the opposite of business as usual. It means looking for better ways to get things done instead of feeling restricted to the way that things have always been done in the past.

- Do your team members think "outside the box"? Effective leaders encourage their team members to think creatively and develop more effective ways of getting things done.

- Are you more committed to a vision or an ideal than to an organization?

- Do you make others feel important and look for ways to compliment and reward them?

- Do you live by what Tony Alessandra calls the "platinum rule"[2]? Living by the golden rule means treating others like you want to be treated. Living by the platinum rule means treating others the way they want to be treated.

- Do you exercise self-control? Set a good example for your team members by restraining yourself.

- Are you a good communicator? Effective leaders have good oral, written, and technological skills. Remember that communication is less about speaking and more about listening. The correct ratio is approximately four to one: Spend about four times as much time listening as talking.

- Do you admit your mistakes? Doing so sends a positive message. Besides, most problems don't go away on their own. Most are solved by communication.

- Do you stay close to the action without getting involved in every, single detail? Little things often make a big difference, but effective leaders focus on the things that are truly important. Know what you need to know and stay informed.

- Are you independent, self-assured, and goal oriented?

- Are you daring enough to take calculated risks? You can't get to second base if you don't take your foot off first base. Although effective leaders don't win every time they take a risk, they typically win more often than they lose.

- Are you focused on winning? Analyze what you did wrong when you lose and what you did right when you win.

- Do you have a high energy level? Because high stress saps energy, effective leaders typically practice effective stress management.

- Do you know how to empower others to achieve success? Because

---

[2]Alessandra, T., and O'Connor, M.J., *The Platinum Rule.* New York: Warner Books, Inc., 1996.

motivation comes from within, you can't really motivate someone else. You can, however, create a climate that motivates others. Sometimes a simple change is all it takes to nudge people into doing something well that they haven't been doing at all.

- Do you have a sense of humor? Humor can heal and can reduce stress in you and your team. Remember, the shortest distance between two people is a smile. And a smile is a curve that sets everything straight.

- Are you a visible presence? Effective leaders show themselves and their positive interest in project outcomes.

- Are you committed to what you do?

- Do you rely on respect rather than popularity? Remember, you can't please all the people all the time. Your emphasis should be on becoming a strong and effective leader rather than a good colleague.

- Are you sincerely concerned about the welfare of the people you're leading?

- Are you adaptable?

- Are you service-minded?

- Are you optimistic?

- Are you decisive?

- Are you open to change and new ideas?

- Are you ethical?

- Are you trustworthy and trusting?

- Are you creative?

- Do you lead by example? Effective leaders are also good role models.

- Do you treat people with respect and dignity?

- Are you supportive of others when that's appropriate?

- Do you evaluate yourself critically and do the same for others?

- Have you prepared yourself extremely well for your position?

- Do you initiate change?

- Do you nurture future managers and leaders? The best football coaches prepare their best assistant coaches for head coach positions. The best leaders also prepare their best team members for leadership positions.

- Do you provide opportunities for personal growth to your team members and do the same for yourself? Effective leaders look for talented team members and are pleased with their successes.

- Do you share knowledge instead of hoarding it? Effective leaders instruct, rather than expect subordinates to guess how tasks are to be done.

- Are you competitive?

- Are you resilient?

- Are you inquisitive?

- Are you influential?

- Are you attentive?

- Do you take advantage of opportunities?

- Do you scan and focus? Effective leaders keep their outlook broad but focus in on what's important. Doing so will help you sense changes in your environment and respond more quickly.

- Do you see patterns where others do not?

- Are you a good teacher?

- Do you use technology appropriately? Computers, e-mail, and other technological innovations threaten to overwhelm us with data. But to lead effectively, you have to understand and use technology. It's no longer funny when organizational leaders boast that they refuse to learn how to use a computer. They're sending the message that they are dinosaurs willing to put their companies at risk.

- Do you welcome constructive criticism? Some managers avoid asking for criticism, because they think it makes them look weak. Don't be one of them. Use feedback as a way to improve your performance. You'll find yourself constantly growing and improving.

Now that you've had a moment to reflect on your leadership skills, select several of the characteristics listed above and set goals for incorporating them into your life. Spend some time every week working toward these goals. But first, let's look at some tips for developing effective goals. The next chapter addresses the first step toward success: putting balance in your life with written goals.

• *Chapter Two* •

Putting Balance in Your Life With Written Goals

Most people aim at nothing in life and hit it with amazing accuracy.
—Zig Ziglar

The first time I met the legendary University of Alabama football coach Paul "Bear" Bryant, he asked me what year I had graduated from the university. I proudly informed him that I had graduated in 1961. "Ah, a very good year," he said smiling. I didn't understand what that comment meant and spent several days completely baffled. Then a light went on. I finally remembered that it was 1961 when Alabama had won the National College Football Championship title for the first time.

Every year, Coach Bryant would write down his goal of winning the title. In 1961, the team achieved that goal. Over the course of his 25-year tenure at the University of Alabama, his team achieved that goal five more times. Of course, that meant that Coach Bryant failed to reach his goal 19 times. Another goal he wrote down each year was to win the Southeastern Football Championship title. His team won that title 13 times, meaning that the coach failed to reach that goal 12 times.

Did these failures make Coach Bryant a failure? Hardly. As a coach at a top university, he won more football games than any other major college coach in football history. The truth is, we don't always achieve all of our goals. But if we don't have goals, we achieve even less.

Winning football championships was Coach Bryant's goal. What is yours? Coach Bryant used to tell his players, "Have goals, have a plan to reach your goals, and stick to your plan." Don't allow other people, such as a spouse, parent, or child, set your goals. Even at work, your employer's goals should simply serve as a guide to your own goals. You need to determine what's really important to you in each of the important areas of your life: mental, physical, spiritual, social, financial, career, and family.

Goals

Most people spend more time planning a one-week vacation than they do planning their lives! Most people know what they don't want, but don't know what they do want. And they certainly don't have written goals. Successful people do, however. After all, you can't score without a goal line. A goal is an idea directed to a desired result, a way of making your dreams come true. And writing goals down is important. Unless you write them down, goals are simply wishes or dreams.

Remember that your goals are only written on paper, not etched in stone. Don't feel that you are setting a permanent course for your life. Life is a process that changes constantly. You may need to change your goals as your situation changes. And by the time you achieve a goal, you may find that other goals seem more or less important. Change your goals to reflect your changing values, experiences, and desires.

Benefits of Having—and Achieving—Goals

Here are some of the many benefits of having and achieving goals:

• You will know, be, do, and have more.

• You will use your mind and talents more effectively.

• You will have more purpose and direction in your life.

• You will make better decisions.

• You will be more organized and effective.

• You will do more for yourself and others.

• You will have higher self-esteem.

• You will boost your motivation.

Your Wants

Before you start setting goals, write down what you have ever wanted to be, do, or have. Then write down why you want these things. As you prepare your list, you may find it convenient to think about the following categories:

• Career

• Leisure

• Finances

• Education

• Religion

• Children

• Travel

• Leadership

• Health and fitness

• Auto

• Personal development

• Social life

• Family

• Friendships

Balance

After several days of evaluating the list of wants you created above, you'll have a good idea of what's important to you. Shorten the list, making sure that you achieve balance in the following areas of your life:

• Physical

- Financial

- Mental

- Family

- Spiritual

- Social

- Career

Types of Goals

There are two basic types of goals:

- Give up goals, such as losing weight, quitting smoking, or stopping your habit of being late to work

- Group goals, such as becoming your company's safety expert, obtaining your professional certification, or becoming your departmental manager when the current manager retires next year

Effective Goals

Follow these rules for developing effective goals:

- Put goals in writing. Writing a goal down clarifies it.

- Make your goals specific. "Become rich" is not specific. "Accumulate a net worth of $1.2 million by age 59" is.

- Make your goals believable, realistic, and achievable. You should know what it takes on a daily basis to achieve your goal.

- Quantify your goals whenever possible. You have to be able to measure your goal to know if you've achieved it.

- Balance the need to make your goals realistic and achievable with the need to make them challenging.

- Make your goals flexible enough to adjust to changing conditions.

- Include your loved ones in your goals.

- Make sure that your goals don't conflict with each other.

- Review your goals every day. Keeping your list of goals in a datebook organizer is convenient and helpful.

- Give yourself target dates for completing your goals. Goals without time schedules quickly become daydreams.

- Make your goals long-term. Objectives are what you do every day as part of your plan for reaching your goals. Goals should have a longer horizon.

Examples

Here are some examples of effective goals:

- By the time I retire 11 years from now, I will have a net worth of $1.2 million.

- I will earn my professional certification by November 1 of next year.

- Four years from now I will be the manager of my department.

- Thirty days from today I will no longer smoke.

- I will pay off my mortgage in eight years by making double payments in February, May, July, and October each year.

- Starting on Monday, I will spend one hour a day getting better at what I do.

Most people don't have written goals! To become a goal-oriented person, you have to change your habits.

Obstacles

Knowing how not to do something brings you closer to knowing how to do something right. In my quest for success, I like to study how not to do things. When it comes to achieving goals, I've noticed six reasons people fail:

• Failure to put goals in writing, set deadlines, make goals realistic, or follow the other guidelines for developing effective goals

• Procrastination

• Failure to divide the plan for reaching goals into small units

• Fear of failure

• Lack of self-confidence

• Lack of discipline

In the next chapter, you'll learn how to create a plan for reaching your goals — and stick to it.

• *Chapter Three* •

Creating a Plan for Reaching Your Goals — and Sticking to It

No one can predict what heights you can soar to. Even you will not know until you spread your wings.

—Author Unknown

Goal-setting is important, but goal-doing is even more important. Most of us have many more things to do than we can possibly accomplish each day. Successful people set priorities; unsuccessful people perform random activities. As you create a plan for reaching your goals, you must decide what to do and what not to do.

Reaching Your Goals

Reaching a goal is a nine-step process:

1. Identify your goal and put it in writing.

2. Set a realistic deadline for achieving the goal.

3. List obstacles that you must overcome to reach your goal.

4. Identify people and resources that can help you achieve your goal.

5. List the skills and knowledge you must use or acquire to reach your goal.

6. Develop a plan of action that breaks your goal down into achievable segments. It's much easier to stay motivated if you can visualize the steps you'll need to get there.

7. List the benefits that achieving your goal will bring you. If there aren't any benefits, you won't work to reach that goal!

8. Make a commitment. If you are constantly noticing the sacrifices you must make to reach your goal, that goal is probably not appropriate for you.

9. Visualize yourself achieving your goal. This step greatly improves your chances of meeting your goal.

Goal Plan

The template on the following pages should help you prepare a plan for reaching each of your goals. Feel free to make copies of the template for your personal use. Following the template are three sample goal plans that can help you as you write your own plan.

Goal Plan

My goal is:

I will complete this goal by:

The benefits of achieving this goal include:

-
-
-
-
-

Obstacles I must overcome to reach this goal include:

-
-
-
-
-

Additional skills and knowledge I must acquire to achieve this goal include:

-
-
-
-
-

People and resources that can help me reach this goal include:

-
-
-
-
-

My action plan for achieving this goal includes the following steps:

-
-
-
-
-

I commit to achieving this goal. I will stick to my plan.

Signature:_____   Date:_____

Goal Plan Example One

My goal is:

   To acquire an up-to-date personal computer with modem

I will complete this goal by:

   Six months from today

The benefits of achieving this goal include:

   • Increased time thanks to the computer's greater speed

   • Increased time thanks to the modem's greater speed

   • Ability to take advantage of new software that won't run on my current computer

   • Ability to take advantage of the Internet's research opportunities

Obstacles I must overcome to reach this goal include:

   • Expense of replacing current software, which is incompatible with the new computer

   • Lack of information about which computer, modem, and software to buy

   • Current computer's lack of trade-in or resale value

   • No foreseeable increase in income

   • Poor money-management skills

   • High monthly payments

Additional skills and knowledge I must acquire to achieve this goal include:

   • Money-management and budgeting skills

- Money-stretching techniques

- Information about getting the best deal on a computer

- Information about choosing appropriate computer hardware and software

People and resources that can help me reach this goal include:

- Bank

- Part-time employer

- Library

- My company's computer or data-processing specialist

My action plan for achieving this goal includes the following steps:

- Record all my expenditures for one month

- Skip out-of-town vacations and deposit the savings that result in an interest-bearing account

- Set up a budget and stick to it

- Listen to audiotapes about dollar-stretching and financial management while driving

- Take a temporary part-time job

- Put pictures of the computer I plan to buy on my bathroom mirror, on my refrigerator door, and in my datebook organizer

I commit to achieving this goal. I will stick to my plan.

Signature:_____   Date:_____

Goal Plan Example Two

My goal is:

   To double the amount of my savings account

I will complete this goal by:

   The end of the year

The benefits of achieving this goal are:

   • Financial independence

   • Freedom from debt

   • Ability to retire early if I want

Obstacles I must overcome to reach this goal are:

   • Practice of using credit cards for purchases and not paying off balances within 30 days

   • Expensive habits like eating out too often, buying a new car every three years, and vacationing in faraway places

   • Tendency to spend bonuses and raises as soon as I receive them

Additional skills and knowledge I must acquire to achieve this goal include:

   • Budgeting skills

   • Saving skills

   • Tips on reducing expenses

People and resources that can help me reach this goal include:

   • Accountant

- Banker

- Books, audiotapes, and videotapes on financial planning

My action plan for achieving this goal includes the following steps:

- Save credit cards for emergency use only

- Make a list of my credit card debts and pay them off one by one

- Make bigger down payments or pay cash for purchases whenever possible

- Put money from raises, bonuses, overtime, gifts, and paid-off loans into a savings account to prevent it from disappearing into routine living expenses

- Contribute the maximum amount possible to my company-sponsored 401(k) plan or to my Keogh plan

- Find low-cost entertainment and vacation options by exploring my own area and enjoying local museums, historical attractions, and lectures

- Keep my car for at least six years before buying a new one

- Avoid restaurant lunches and vending machine purchases by bringing lunch, snacks, and drinks from home

I commit to achieving this goal. I will stick to my plan.

Signature:_____   Date:_____

Goal Plan Example Three

My goal is:

To obtain my professional certification

I will complete this goal by:

Eighteen months from today

The benefits of achieving this goal are:

- Increased opportunity for work advancement

- Increased self-esteem

- Increased confidence in my future

- Higher income

- Greater job security

Obstacles I must overcome to reach this goal include:

- Heavy family demands

- Lack of self-confidence, especially when it comes to taking tests

- After-work fatigue that makes studying hard

Additional skills and knowledge I must acquire to achieve this goal include:

- Time management skills

- Information about taking tests more successfully

- Positive mental attitude

- Study skills

People and resources that can help me reach this goal include:

- Books, journals, audiotapes, and videotapes from the library

- Employer

- Mentor

My action plan for achieving this goal includes the following steps:

- Secure my family's support

- Listen to instructional and motivational tapes on time management, test-taking, and study skills while driving

- Budget time for studying technical material in my daily plan

- Attend seminars and workshops on the material covered in the certification exam

- Increase my energy by walking 30 minutes during my lunch hour four days a week, rain or shine

- Limit television-viewing to two hours a week until I achieve my goal

I commit to achieving this goal. I will stick to my plan.

Signature:_____   Date:_____

Prioritization

Most of us have more things to do each day than we can possibly accomplish. Prioritization is the process of valuing. If you fail to plan, you are in effect planning to fail! Each hour you spend planning can save you three to four hours down the road. Plus, you'll achieve better results.

Keep in mind the difference between efficiency and effectiveness. Efficiency means doing the job right, but effectiveness means doing the right job efficiently. Many people spend their time working on the wrong thing. Goals, prioritization, and scheduling serve as a rudder that steers us in the right direction. Without a rudder, our sailboat goes whatever way the wind is blowing. In real life, that means you spend your time managing crises rather than getting real work done.

Another thing to keep in mind is the 20-80 rule originated by Vilfredo Pareto, who noted that 80 percent of a reward comes from 20 percent of the effort. Identifying that 20 percent is the key to successful prioritization. If your to-do list includes 10 items and you do the right two, you will have completed 80 percent of your work.

Prioritize in a way that makes sense to you. One convenient method is to assign each task the letter "A", "B", "C", or "D." "A" priorities are vitally important. "B" priorities are important. "C" priorities have some value. "D" priorities have no real value. Then work first things first. Spend most of your time on "A"s and "B"s. That way, you will have gotten the most important things done even if you run out of time. Do your "C"s only if you have time, and don't do your "D"s at all.

Use your datebook organizer to keep track of your priorities. Make out a to-do list at the end of each day, then review it the following morning. Practically everything you do should be in your datebook organizer. Think of it as your tool for controlling events and activities. Don't leave home without it!

In the next chapter, you'll learn how to plan for the unexpected and become a master of change.

• *Chapter Four* •

Expecting the Unexpected and Becoming a Master of Change

It is not the strongest of species that survive, nor the most intelligent, but the one that is most responsive to change.
—Charles Darwin

The dinosaur doesn't exist today, because it couldn't change and it couldn't adapt. Therefore, the dinosaur became extinct. We will become extinct in the 21st century if we are not able to change and adapt!
—Christopher S. Frings

The Changing Workplace

Three things have acted as catalysts for all the change in this country: cost, technology, and politics.

We are in the middle of a true revolution in terms of how work gets done, the third such revolution in civilization's history. The first was the Agricultural Revolution. In the period between about 8,000 B.C. and the late 1600s, we moved from hunting and gathering to growing food. Next came the Industrial Revolution, during which we started depending on machines to get things done. Pulling levers and pushing buttons replaced much of the heavy lifting we used to do. The third revolution is happening right now. With the development of the computer and improvements in telecommunications around 1950, we entered the Information Age. Work is once again being radically transformed.

In the Information Age, brainpower has replaced horsepower. Work is less physical and more mental; knowledge is more crucial than muscles. Ideas, formulas, and data are replacing things. In fact, things are now made by other things rather than by people. Computers are running assembly lines, and robots are making automobiles.

Computers and modern telecommunication systems are reshaping the work environment. Laptop computers, modems, cellular phones, pagers, and other technologies allow you to work at home, in your car, or anywhere else as easily as you can in your office. This ability means you can enjoy much more job freedom, but it also means that companies can go almost anywhere in the world in search of people willing to work for the lowest salaries.

The Entitlement Mindset

In 1935, the government stepped in with the form of welfare known as Social Security. The intention was good, but the government gave us a crutch we have been leaning on more and more ever since. World War II ended the Depression. The postwar years brought a period of renewed confidence. The economy boomed, and people expressed optimism and pride in the American way. For the next 30 years, politicians and businesses acted and talked like they could create the perfect society. The federal government became extremely generous, and with free spending came ever-growing government programs. Corporate America followed suit with big spending.

We gradually programmed ourselves to believe that big business and big government would protect us. We convinced ourselves that we deserved all that business and government offered us, and that it was our right. The ethic of personal responsibility grew weaker and weaker as we shifted toward an entitlement mindset. We started expecting "our fair share" from our employers and the government. And we actually depended upon corporate America to protect our careers.

In the 1970s, productivity finally stopped growing. Corporate profits dropped below what they had been in the 1950s and 1960s. By the 1980s, panicked business leaders started re-engineering, restructuring, and downsizing. Many jobs disappeared, and the government decided that it also needed to shrink. Because the money was no longer there, companies had to change their spending habits.

The result? Today we find that corporate America cannot guarantee our job security, and the government cannot deliver on politicians' promises. Welfare is being drastically reformed. Our paradigm must shift from entitlement to earning and from rights to responsibilities.

This thumbnail sketch of change explains how we got to the turbulent late 1990s. And it suggests that we can expect even more change in the 21st century.

Take product life cycles. In 1990, for instance, it took six years to bring an automobile from concept to production. Today it takes two. In some companies, the product life cycle is even faster. Most of Hewlett Packard's revenues come from products that didn't even exist a year ago.

Businesses have changed the way they want to do business. In response, workers are changing the way they work. The corporate ladder has been replaced by team-based organizations, for instance. And workers are trading flex-time, telecommuting, and other arrangements for the nine-to-five grind of working in the same place for the same boss. Employers have finally recognized that a leaner, more efficient staff leads to a better bottom line. Experts predict that 85 percent of workers will be employed by small businesses by the year 2020 and that 50 percent will find themselves in non-traditional work arrangements. These arrangements will include temporary employment. In fact, "temps" are already one of the fastest growing employment categories. New technology will cause further change.

These changes upset many people. Yet we cause progress, because we are tough customers. When companies restructure, outsource, merge, downsize, or go out of business altogether, ordinary people like you and me often have a hand in it. As customers, we cause change. That's the American way.

Resisting change is a no win battle. Don't waste your time defending old ways of doing things. Instead, start figuring out how your job and profession are changing and how tomorrow's tools and methods will further alter the way you work. Investing your own money and time in developing your skills is crucial. Remember, the most powerful asset in the Information Age is knowledge. And what you need to know is changing all the time. The biggest challenge today is not getting an education, it's keeping one! In three years, at least half of your skills will be outdated. The good news is that knowledge has never been easier to acquire. Technology grows more user-friendly every day. While the Industrial Age was about powerful organizations, the Information Age is about powerful individuals who wield information.

These days you probably can't keep your job simply by "keeping your nose clean" and "holding down the fort." You have to do more! Remember, you are responsible for your own success. You have to make your own work succeed. Part of your job is to make your services or products obsolete before your competitor does. In the Information Age, everyone must be an innovator.

Change Isn't Easy

When anyone complains to me about change, I tell them this story. In 1829, then-governor Martin Van Buren wrote to the President. "The canal system of this country is being threatened by the spread of a new form of transportation known as railroads," he wrote. "As you may well know, railroad carriages are pulled at the enormous speed of 15 miles per hour by engines, which, in addition to endangering the life and limbs of passengers, roar and snort their way through the countryside. The Almighty certainly never intended that people should travel at such breakneck speed."

When was the last time you changed your behavior? There's an old saying that goes like this: If you always do what you have always done, you will always get what you have always got. That's no longer true. Today doing only what you have done in the past means that you will get left behind. To increase your productivity these days, you will have to change at least some of your behavior. Think about it. The best supervisors, managers, and leaders are masters of change. In fact, a manager's most important survival skill is the ability to anticipate change and identify new opportunities. You have to become receptive to change, too. I even keep a plastic dinosaur on my desk to remind myself that failing to change will guarantee my extinction.

When a new idea comes into being, it's often not the content but people's attitudes toward it that matter. Here's an easy way to illustrate that point. Use your non-dominant hand to write the word "attitude" on a sheet of paper. Does it look awkward and incompetent? That's because you were outside your comfort zone when you wrote it. That scrawled word gives you a picture of the attitude we often have when we try something new, especially if that change was imposed upon us. That's because first-time experiences threaten our security. When you are asked to make a change or someone asks you to learn something new, remember the difference between writing with your usual hand and writing with your non-dominant hand.

You can change yourself if you can change what goes into your mind. Although it's true that every improvement is the result of change, not every change is an improvement. The past has value, and it will continue to have value. At the same time, you shouldn't let the past have a veto. Take the best from the past and the best from the future to make success for yourself. The result may mean turmoil, but it's worth it.

Resistance to Change

To cope effectively with change, you have to understand why people often resist it:

Self Interest: People often fear that change will mean they'll lose something they once had. When a new vice president decides to create a new managerial position, for instance, the existing supervisors may resist out of fear that they will lose decision-making power.

Lack of Trust: If people don't trust the person with the new idea, they may suspect that he or she has a hidden agenda. For example, staff members who oppose the idea of flexible scheduling may not trust the personnel manager who suggested the idea.

Differing Viewpoints: Different people will view any change differently.

Fear of Failure: People sometimes resist change because they fear they will be unable to handle new conditions competently.

Fear of Uncertainty: Some people resist change just because it's change. They fear change because they know it will alter their routines. They may be reluctant to give up comfortable work patterns or relationships with co-workers.

Forms of Resistance to Change

People's resistance to change expresses itself in a variety of ways. Here are some of them:

Negativity: "It won't work! We already tried that."

Apathy and indifference: "I just work here."

Pet project attitude: "Are you criticizing my plan?"

Unconscious dissension: "Whatever the boss says... but it won't work."

Translation: "We'll implement my variation; it's better anyway."

Authoritarianism: "Yours is not to reason why..."

Common Changes

The following changes are common today. Which of them have you already experienced? Are you ready for the others listed?

• Change in your professional organization's name

• Change in your company's name

• Technological change

• Reengineering

• Merger

• Acquisition

• Divestiture

• Layoff

• Downsizing

• Launch of new company, division, or department

• Turnover in top management

• New policies, values, or expectations

• Deregulation

• Reorganization

• New competition

• Changes in company benefits

- New management

- Promotion

Looking Ahead

You can expect to see the following changes in many organizations in the future. How many have you already noticed in your organization?

- More employee involvement in all levels of decision-making

- Increased emphasis on meaningful work

- More responsibility for individual employees

- Fewer managers and more participation in self-managed teams

- Greater emphasis on human capital demonstrated by increased investment in training, retraining, and new skill development

- Encouragement of mutual respect and trust

- Growth of employee rights protections

- Continuing demand for workers with good communication skills

- Increased popularity of programs like flex-time that allow workers to balance work and family demands

- Better recognition and reward for superior performance

- Greater diversity in the workplace

- Continuing demand for workers with specialized skills

- Emergence of multi-skilled, cross-trained generalists with specialized skills

- Smaller workspaces for each employee

- Increased use of surveillance tools to maximize productivity and minimize losses

Managing Change

Whether change is major or minor, it typically prompts a similar response. We go through the following four stages in response to change:

1. The first stage is denial. The fact that change is occurring and that it will affect you doesn't sink in right away. A typical response might be, "They can't be merging our laboratory with that laboratory across town." People in this stage tend to focus on the past.

2. The second stage is resistance. In this stage, strong negative feelings about the change emerge. Anger, blame, depression, anxiety, uncertainty, frustration, and self-doubt are common.

3. The third stage is acceptance. During this stage, people draw upon their internal resources to figure out their new responsibilities and visualize their future. This can be exciting if people learn to view change as adventure and opportunity. In this stage, people may be confused about details or concerned about lack of focus.

4. The final stage is commitment to change. It's at this point that people are able to set new goals and make plans for reaching them. People in this stage are typically cooperative and focused as they anticipate their next challenge.

The longer you stay in the denial and resistance stages, the harder and more painful the change will be. Try to get through the denial and resistance stages quickly and move on to a commitment to change. Of course, exchanging something old for something new means the death of the familiar. Even if the change brings something better, you still have to allow time for mourning and recovery.

Overcoming Resistance to Change

Need some ideas for helping people overcome their resistance to change? Below are five situations and ideas for helping people adapt to the changes the situations represent. Of course, these strategies aren't the only way to deal with these situations. The examples are included simply to give you some ideas for handling similar situations.

Example A

Change Situation: Your employees don't have enough accurate information to understand the problem.

Strategy: When making changes, give employees as much information as possible about the change and why you are making it. Be sure to give them this information before you start making changes.

Example: A new laboratory opened. At first the lab hours were 8:00 to 5:30. Some laboratory employees worked from 8:00 to 5:00; others worked from 8:30 to 5:30. After six months, business was booming. To meet the needs of physicians and their patients, the lab manager decided that the lab needed to stay open until 6:30. The manager also decided that only one person needed to be there at 8:00. To make this change, the manager met with all of the employees as soon as this decision was made. He told everyone about the changing needs of the lab's clients and informed them that working hours had to be changed to meet those needs. Giving specific information about the changes, he announced that the change would take place in a month. That gave employees plenty of time to make changes in their transportation and child-care arrangements.

Example B

Change Situation: Your employees have considerable power to resist your proposed change.

Strategy: Allow the people who will be affected by the change to participate in your decision-making. Encouraging people to help you decide what needs to be done and how to do it can be a great team-building opportunity.

Example: A health maintenance organization purchased two hospitals in a large metropolitan area. The company's chief executive officer and chief operating officer didn't want to keep laboratories in both hospitals open. Rumors were flying about when and how the lab-closing would happen. The company appointed a team consisting of two staff members from each lab, an assistant administrator from each hospital, and the medical director from each hospital. The company then gave them two weeks to discuss the matter and prepare a proposal for how the change should be implemented.

Example C

Change Situation: You have considerable power to enforce your ideas and speed is essential.

Strategy: Announce the change and enforce it with authority, certainty, and firmness.

Example: A hospital's chief executive officer, chief operating officer, and laboratory director decided to change testing procedures at the hospital. As a result of the change, a laboratory worker now had to work with the nurses as a troubleshooter, problem solver, quality control coordinator and quality assurance coordinator for the laboratory tests performed by the nurses. This supervisory duty would rotate weekly among the four laboratory workers. Some of these laboratory workers were upset about this change, because it meant that they wouldn't have their usual days off. After hearing their complaints, the laboratory manager called the four of them together and announced that the decision had already been made and that the change would occur as scheduled.

Example D

Change Situation: One of your employees will clearly lose as a result of the change, and he or she has lots of power to resist.

Strategy: Negotiate a win-win solution.

Example: Two laboratories were merging to form one central lab. This merger meant that only one laboratory manager was now needed. The two current lab managers were both productive employees with positive mental attitudes and great team-building skills. Instead of choosing between them, the chief operating officer talked to both of them together and individually. He stressed to both of them how important they were to the new central lab. He then made one of them the manager of the new lab and gave the other one the job of coordinating operations between the central lab and its satellite labs. Both of them were given six percent pay increases.

Example E

Change Situation: People resist your change, because they're not convinced that it will work for them.

Strategy: Help them adjust by making the change as easy and comfortable as possible.

Example: A laboratory worker was upset, because schedule changes seemed to threaten her ability to care for a child with cystic fibrosis. Because her day off had been changed, she would no longer be able to get her son to the clinic on his usual day. She told the lab manager that her parents would be moving near her in two months and would be able to take her son to the clinic for her. Stressing the reason the scheduling change had to be made, the manager gave the employee two months instead of two weeks to make the switch to the new schedule.

Becoming a Change Agent

You can make yourself receptive to change. When you follow the rules below, you are no longer part of the problem but part of the solution. Try these strategies:

• Keep a positive mental attitude.

• Make managing change part of your job description.

• Don't fight losing battles.

• Recognize that upper managers are frequently in uncharted waters. Support them by tolerating their mistakes.

• Keep your sense of humor.

• Refocus rapidly so that your strengths don't turn into weaknesses.

• Remember that worry is the misuse of imagination and practice good stress management.

• Invent the future instead of trying to redesign the past.

• Communicate clearly and directly.

Paradigm Shifts

Every industry is undergoing profound paradigm shifts. Although each industry is experiencing its own unique brand of changes, they share many of them in common. Here are some of the paradigm shifts that are occurring in the health-care arena:

From	*To*
Illness care	Healthcare
Mental illness	Mental health
Competition	Partnerships
Quality control	Continuous quality improvement
Quality assurance	Service excellence
Fragmented services	Integrated care
Departmental focus	Interdisciplinary focus
New technology	Appropriate technology
Fee for service	Managed care
Downsizing	Rightsizing
Boss	Mentor/facilitator/coach
Turf protection	Group production
Revenue from services	Revenue from covered lives
Cost-based competition	Quality-based competition

Economics of scale	Economics of coordination
Activity orientation	Outcome orientation
Task focus	Customer focus
Manager	Leader
Individuals	Teams
Distrust	Trust
Revenue	Cost
Reaction	Initiation
Control	Empowerment
Periodic improvement	Continuous improvement
Fixing blame	Fixing problems
Resisting change	Embracing change

Trends

Expect both the expected and the unexpected. Trends are rapidly changing and so are attitudes, expectations, and roles. More changes are coming. The following is a list of changes you can expect to see in the health-care industry as well as many others. Many are already happening. Which changes are you ready for? What skills do you need to develop to get ready for the others? Our environment is not going to change to please us. Some of us are only rearranging the chairs on the deck of the Titanic!

- Due to the Clinton Administration's proposed health-care reform, health-care professionals are forming alliances with people they previously looked upon as enemies. The health-care industry is reforming itself before mandatory change is imposed.

- The rate of change is increasing.

- Expectations at all levels are rising

- The number of managers is decreasing.

- Costs are being reduced.

- Medical care is being managed, which means reduced test volume, cost containment, rightsizing, capitated reimbursement, reduced reimbursement, and an emphasis on appropriateness when selecting laboratory tests.

- Health-care professionals are being forced to become better managers of their budgets, personnel, businesses, and themselves.

- Opportunities are different, and different skills are required.

- Changes are driven by technology as well as by costs and legislative issues.

- There will be an unprecedented demand for "alternative" therapies, reflecting a trend from institution-managed care to self-managed care.[3] More and more consumers are already turning to therapies such as biofeedback, herbs, prayer, and chiropractic. More than a third of Americans use alternative therapies each year, spending $14 billion—most of it out-of-pocket. Demand will only accelerate, fueled mostly by aging baby boomers' openness to new concepts and consumers' perception that holistic approaches are more natural and less intimidating. This trend toward alternative medicine shouldn't be seen as a threat to conventional medicine but rather as a complement to it.

- According to Gordon Moore, the number of components that can be packed on a computer chip doubles every two years but the price remains the same. Amazingly, this law has held true for more than 30 years. That means that computer power per dollar doubles every

---

[3]*Trend Letter*, Volume 16: Number 1, September 4, 1997.

two years. Although Moore's law will probably not hold true forever, in the meantime you should recognize that improved technology renders personal computers obsolete about every three years. Although you don't have to replace your screen, keyboard, mouse, printer, and other accessories, treat your computer as disposable and replace it every three years or so.

• Most workers are expected to increase their personal productivity and that of their teams.

Competing in Tomorrow's Health-Care Arena

How can you master change? Here are a few tips for gaining control of your destiny in the health-care arena and others:

• Get involved.

• Be part of the solution, not part of the problem.

• Demonstrate your worth.

• Develop positive relationships.

• Expect and prepare for the expected.

• Lead the technological revolution.

• Keep a positive mental attitude.

• Make managing change part of your job description.

• Don't fight losing battles.

• Be tolerant of management's mistakes.

• Keep (or develop) a sense of humor.

• Refocus rapidly so that your strengths don't turn into weaknesses.

- Remember that worry is the misuse of imagination and practice effective stress management.

- Support upper management.

- Initiate or join cross-functional teams.

- Invent the future instead of trying to rediscover the past.

- Anticipate revolutions in the health-care industry and build your capabilities now so that you can win in the future.

- Look three to five years in the future.

- Be proactive instead of constantly reacting to each new competitive threat as it comes along.

- Become different.

- Shape your industry's future.

Another way to take charge of your future is to spend time now building the skills you'll need down the road. These skills include the following:

- Financial management

- Cost analysis

- Budgeting

- Returns on investments

- Break-even analysis

- Outcomes assessment and analysis

- Continuous quality improvement and total quality improvement

- Resource management and utilization allocation

• Personnel

• Materials

• Self-management and personal development skills

• Goal-setting

• Time management

• Change management

• Stress management

• Team-building

• Negotiation skills

• Presentation skills

• Informatics (systems, reporting, and telecommunications)

• Risk assessment and management

• Regulatory issues and laws affecting your industry

Are you still resisting change? Use a rubber band to snap out of it! Some of my clients wear rubber bands around their wrists as self-motivators. When they feel themselves resisting change, they snap out of it by snapping the rubber band. The sensation reminds them to move actively through the denial and resistance stages so that they can make change happen positively.

In the next chapter, you'll find out how to learn from your mistakes.

• *Chapter Five* •

Learning From Past Mistakes and Successes

You must learn from the mistakes of others. You can't possibly live long enough to make them all yourself.

—Sam Levenson

You are either the creature of circumstance or the creator of circumstance.

—Mark Victor Hansen

The concept of learning from your mistakes—and your successes—is just common sense. But common sense isn't practiced often enough! How many times have you made the same mistake twice? Proper planning and goal-setting will help you make better decisions next time.

You can learn a lot from other people's mistakes and successes, too. Don't ask star performers what makes them successful. Watch them! Often they're not even aware of the real keys to their success. Pay attention to what they do, not what they say. Great achievers don't have a magic formula. They are super-achievers because they set exciting goals, make maximum use of their creativity, and don't let problems overwhelm them. They never give up. Most people can follow their example.

Many of the methods super-achievers used in the past are still useful today. Occasionally ask yourself who you would talk to if you could spend seven days asking questions of seven of the greatest people who ever lived. Once you've identified your heroes, find out more about them. Learn how they became successful and find ways to use the same strategies in your own life. Change your list of super-achievers from time to time. As you learn more about some of them, your opinions may change.

You may want to read up on this subject. I recommend Dan Burrus' book *Technotrends: How to Use Technology to Go Beyond the*

Competition[4], which contains 31 key rules. Also take a look at S.R. Covey's book *The Seven Habits of Highly Effective People*[5].

Team Member Needs

According to Coach Paul "Bear" Bryant, winning team members need five things:

1. Tell them what you expect from them.

2. Give them an opportunity to perform.

3. Let them know how they are doing.

4. Give them guidance when they need it.

5. Reward them according to the contributions they make.

Coach Bryant's strategies still work today. Try them and see for yourself.

Hiring and Retaining Good Workers

In a *USA Today* article[6], J.W. Marriott, Jr., chief executive officer of Marriott International, gave some great tips on hiring and retaining good workers:

1. Mix with employees and make yourself seen. Keeping workers happy doesn't mean hiding in your office but walking among employees to gauge their mood.

---

[4]Burrus, Dan, *Technotrends: How to Use Technology to Go Beyond the Competition*. New York: HarperCollins, 1993.

[5]Covey, S.R., *The Seven Habits of Highly Effective People*. New York: Simon & Schuster, 1990.

[6]*USA Today*, September 15, 1997.

2. Listen and respond to employees' complaints. Use confidential surveys regularly. Take action when problems arise.

3. Promote from within whenever possible. The best employees will stay on board if they see opportunities.

You can learn a lot from your failures if you don't become bitter and if you're willing to acknowledge your responsibility. Most people find it extremely difficult to acknowledge their mistakes. Remember that failure is part of being human. A person is not a failure; the activity or event is the failure.

The table on the next page summarizes how 15 people rank the importance of various achievement factors. Use the last column to give your own ratings.

In the next chapter, you'll learn how to use good time management skills to work smarter.

Factors:
Ranked from 0 to 10
or: L (low)
M (moderate)
H (high)

Factor	Robert Shaw	Norman V. Peale	Sandra Day O'Connor	Stanley Marcus	Jack Lemmon	Janet Leigh	Kris Kristofferson	Harry Hoffman	Malcolm Forbes	Erskine Caldwell	Helen Gurley Brown	Isaac Asimov	Mary Kay Ash	Julie Andrews	Hank Aaron	RATE YOURSELF
Time consciousness	9	8	10	9	8	8	8	10	9	10	9	10	9	6	10	
Time management	9	8	10	7	8	10	4	10	8	9	9	8	9	7	10	
Flexibility	4	7	10	7	8	5		10	8	9	6	3	9	7	10	
Focus	9	10	10	8	10	9	10	9	9	9	8	9	9	9	8	
Intensity	9	10	10	4	10	5	10	7	9	9	10	9	10	9		
Breadth of knowledge	5	10	10	6	7	4	10	10	8	1	10	10	4	6	0	
Competence	9	8	M	9	8	H	10	10	H	5	9	10	10	4	10	
Small details	8	7	10		9	9	10	7	6	10	4	5	10	7	8	
How important is:																
The good teacher	8	8	H	10	9	10	10	9	9	1	6	1	10	8	10	
The lucky break	7	10	10	10	4	10	6	9	10	5	7	3	8	10	10	
Being in the right place		10	M		4	6	10	9	10	10	5	8	0	10	10	
A discoverer in your career	8	5	1	0	4	10	8	9	0	9	3	1	0	7	10	
A mentor	7	7	10	0	9	10	10		10	3	5	0	9	6	10	
Reading	7	10	10	10	5	5	10	9		9	9	0	0	8	7	
Travel	7	10	L	10	7	3	10		10	10	5	7	9	8	0	
Nerve, chutzpah	7	8	H	10	9	8	10	8	8	2	7	0	9	5	0	
Desire for recognition	3	4	M	7	8	6	10	10	1	10	5	0	0	8	6	
A feeling of inferiority	7		M	10	5	10	10	10	7	10	10	8	8	0	10	
Desire for self-improvement		10	10	10	8	9	10	8	9	5	7	6	10	8	0	
The challenge itself	8	10	10	10	8	10	10	10	6	5	5	8	8	10	7	
A sense of playfulness	9	7	L	10	10	10	10	5	9	9	10	10	4	9	0	
Creativity	8	5	H	10	10	10	10		6	10	10	5	10	10	0	
Discipline	5	10	M	3	8	4	10	5		10	7	0	8	10	10	
Economic incentives at beginning of career	9			7	3	9	0	4			9	5	6	10	10	
Today	8	4	L	7	8	9	10	5	5	10	10	3	7	5	7	
How teachable are you?	1	10	H	8	10	9	10	9	5	10	7	8	8	6	7	
Are you a good listener?	5	10	H	8	10	9	10	10	4	10	9	10	9	7	10	
How brave are you?	8	10		5	10	3	10	7		10	10	10	10	8	10	
How persistent are you?	8	10	M	6	10	5	10	10	8	10	5	9	9	9	10	
How self-confident are you?	2	8	H	9	8	10	10	10	8	10	8	10	10	4	10	
How much do you enjoy your work?	9	10	10	10	10	10	10	10	10	10	9	10	10	9	10	

Table is used by permission of Eugene Griessman and is excerpted from his book The Achievement Factors, *Pfeiffer, © 1990, 1993. Dr. Gene Griessman is an international speaker presenting programs on achievement and time management. He may be reached at 1-800-749-GOAL.*

• *Chapter Six* •

Working Smarter by Using Time Management Techniques

Wasting just one hour a day means that in 10 years you will have lost 3,650 hours or 152 days of your life.
—Christopher S. Frings

Webster's defines time as a sequence of events, one after another. My favorite definition of time is, "Time is the way we spend our lives." If you waste your time, you waste your life. You really cannot manage time. We have 24 hours in every day. What you do with your time is your choice. So time management is really a misnomer. We don't manage time; we manage activities and make choices. Time management means managing activities or events. Good time management means getting full value for your time. Why is managing time important? Time is our most priceless resource. You can use it or waste it. There is always time for important things!

The phrase "spending time" is an accurate one. You only have a certain amount of time to spend. We all have the same amount to spend each day. Spend it well. One thing's for sure: You'll spend your time doing something. The only question is whether you want to control your time or whether you want your time to control you. When you don't take charge, time takes over by default. Effective time management means working smarter, not necessarily harder. As technology makes everything seem more urgent, time management has become more important than ever before.

The Requirements of Effective Time Management

You need two things in order to practice effective time management. First, you need a system. This book gives you practical strategies for practicing effective time management. By the time you finish reading it, you'll know how to start with goals, develop a plan for reaching them, and use your datebook organizer to stay on track. For more information on this topic, refer to my book *The Hitchhiker's Guide to Effective Time Management*[7].

You also need discipline. Your commitment, desire, and attitude will determine whether or not you will use this information to work smarter.

Signs of Poor Time Management

Do you have bad habits when it comes to time management? Here are some of the most common signs of poor time management:

• Rushing

• Chronic vacillation between unpleasant alternatives

• Fatigue coupled with lots of nonproductive activity

• Constantly missed deadlines

• Insufficient time for rest or personal relationships

• Feelings of being overwhelmed by demands, deadlines, and having to do what you don't want to do much of the time

Increasing Your Productivity

Good time management sets off a chain reaction. Effective time management boosts your self-esteem. Increased self-esteem increases your productivity. When you practice effective time management, you set in motion a positive cycle of increased self-esteem and increased productivity. But effective time management requires planning and flexibility. Here are 10 tips to get you started:

---

[7]Christopher S. Frings, *The Hitchhiker's Guide to Effective Time Management*. Washington, DC: AACC Press, 1997.

1. Set goals that put balance in the important areas of your life and have a written plan for reaching them. Goals give direction to each day—and to your life as a whole. Without goals, you cannot practice effective time management. Ask yourself whether what you are about to do will help you accomplish one of your goals in life.

2. Put each day's tasks in priority order and use a daily plan to keep on track. Remember, each hour of planning will save you many hours down the road. Concentrate your efforts on "A" and "B" priorities, and you'll find yourself accomplishing more than ever before.

3. Avoid the tyranny of the urgent. Know that saying, "A lack of proper planning on your part does not constitute an emergency on my part"? Make that your motto as you strive for maximal effectiveness. Urgent tasks usually have short-term consequences, but important tasks have long-term implications in terms of your goals. Work to reduce urgency in your life, so that you have time for truly important priorities.

4. Learn to delegate effectively. Delegation means getting things done through others. The best definition of a good leader is the same as the definition of a chemical catalyst: A catalyst causes things to happen without being used up. If you don't delegate, you will soon use yourself up. And if you don't delegate well, you will find yourself immersed in crisis management. Remember that delegation never absolves you of responsibility. You are still accountable.

5. Pay attention to important details, but avoid routine details. Minimize them, consolidate them, delegate them, or simply eliminate them if possible.

6. Don't spread yourself too thin. "No" is the most powerful time-saving word in the English language. It's a small word, but it can be hard to say. Learn to say no diplomatically and firmly when you're asked to do something that doesn't contribute to your goals. Note that your motivation is not to shirk work but to save time that will allow you to achieve your goals more effectively. When you start saying no to unimportant things, life gets easier.

7. Control interruptions. Whenever possible, establish periods during the day when you won't tolerate interruptions. Keep your schedule

flexible so that an interruption or two doesn't ruin your day. When you expect to be interrupted, schedule routine tasks.

8. Take maximum advantage of new technology. Use your computer, tape recorder, videocassette recorder, fax machine, voice mail, cellular phone, e-mail, modem, autodialer, and the Internet to get things done fast. Listen to instructional and motivational audiotapes while driving or waiting in lines, for instance. Tape a presentation and play it back to find ways of enhancing the real thing.

9. Strive for excellence, but don't be a perfectionist. There's a difference between striving for excellence and striving for perfection. Excellence is attainable, gratifying, and healthy. Perfection is often unattainable, immobilizing, and frustrating. Trying to achieve perfection frequently costs us more time than the increased benefits justify. Of course, we all want to do the job right. But none of us is perfect. When you expect perfection in yourself and others, you are making a big mistake. Pursuing perfection is all right in some circumstances. If you're performing a medical test in your laboratory, filing your income tax return, programming a computer, or building a bridge, for instance, you really do need perfection. But perfection isn't necessary for most of what we do.

10. Control procrastination. Procrastination is the habit of indecision. To control it, visualize an activity's end result rather than the activity itself. Divide and conquer by breaking big tasks into smaller, more manageable units. Create an environment that's conducive to getting the job done. And use to-do lists effectively.

Common Time Wasters

People waste an average of two hours a day by indulging in their five favorite time-wasters. The first step in controlling your time-wasters is identifying them. Act now! Use the list below to identify your top five time-wasters:

- Telephone interruptions
- Drop-in visitors
- Meetings

- Inability to say no
- Leaving tasks unfinished
- Lack of self-discipline

- Crisis management
- Lack of objectives
- Lack of priorities
- Lack of deadlines
- Cluttered desk
- Personal disorganization
- Ineffective delegation
- Attempting too much
- Unrealistic time estimates
- Confused responsibility
- Watching television
- Failure to have a place for things
- Disorganized spouse

- Junk mail
- Losing things
- Conflicting instructions
- Lack of a check-list
- Long lunch hours
- Travel and driving time
- Daydreaming
- Excessive socializing
- Failure to perform tasks correctly
- Lack of clear communication
- Surfing the Web
- Procrastination

Controlling Time-Wasters

Here are some tips to help you control the time-wasters listed above.

Telephone Interruptions:

- Answer, "How can I help you?" rather than, "How are you?"

- When you're busy, let voice mail or another person answer your calls if it's appropriate.

- When a caller is too long-winded or calls when you are working on a higher priority, cut the person off politely and diplomatically by explaining that you have a time constraint, such as a meeting to attend or someone in your office, that prevents you from talking. Suggest a time when you'll be able to talk. Note: Use this tip only when it's appropriate and always tell the truth!

Inability to Say No:

• If you have a reason for saying no, give the reason.

• Offer the person another way to meet his or her objective.

• Keep in mind that saying no has four steps: listening, saying no, giving reasons, and offering alternatives.

Drop-in Visitors:

• When someone comes into your office, stand up and keep standing up. It's polite and will shorten the visitor's stay.

• Set a time limit at the outset. Say something like, "Sure, I can help you with that, but I've got to leave at 10:15."

• When someone drops in, say, "I need 15 minutes to wrap up this report. I'll come to your office then."

• Try working in an unused conference room, an empty office, the library, or the cafeteria before or after mealtimes. No one will know where you are, so you won't have drop-in visitors and other interruptions.

• When you see that a visit is going to go on longer than you expected, say, "I thought this was going to be a short question. I should have asked you how long it was going to take. I have a 1:00 deadline to meet for my team leader. Can we reschedule this for tomorrow at 4:15?"

• Encourage appointments rather than unscheduled visits.

• Rearrange your furniture so that you aren't facing the door.

• Remove any extra chairs from your office.

- Close your door.

- Don't make unnecessary conversation.

- Keep a record of your interruptions.

Leaving Tasks Unfinished:

- Prioritize the tasks on the to-do list in your datebook organizer.

- Work on "A" priorities first. That way you will have completed the important things on your list if you run out of time.

- Complete a task before putting it aside.

Meetings:

- Don't hold a meeting if a phone conversation will suffice.

- When you do hold a meeting, require everyone to be prepared.

- Have a written, prioritized agenda and stick to it.

- Start meetings on time and end early or on time.

Lack of Self-Discipline:

- Have written goals and a plan for reaching them.

- Stick to your plan.

- Make a to-do list in your datebook organizer.

Crisis Management:

- Remember that it's much more efficient to head off problems before they develop.

- Expect the unexpected.

- Have a plan for everything that can go wrong.

- Have a priority list of important tasks that must be handled in advance.

- Focus on long-term plans and consequences whenever possible and defer tasks that only appear urgent on the surface.

- Learn to question the urgent and realize that many things only appear to need immediate attention.

Junk Mail:

- Open your mail over a garbage can.

- Make junk mail a "D" priority.

- Don't handle junk mail more than once.

Lack of Objectives:

- Develop written goals.

- Develop objectives to serve as a plan for reaching your goals.

Losing Things:

- List the things you often have trouble finding.

- Write down where you plan to keep those items in the future and always put them in the places you have identified.

Lack of Priorities:

- Have a prioritized to-do list and stick to it.

- Prepare a to-do list in your datebook organizer at the end of each day.

Conflicting Instructions:

- Make certain that you are clear about what is expected of you when your manager delegates something to you.

- Make an extra effort to ensure that other people involved also understand what's expected.

- Summarize your understanding of the situation.

Lack of Deadlines:

- Set realistic deadlines for all items when you make your to-do list at the end of each day.

Lack of a Check-List:

- Prepare a to-do list in your datebook organizer at the end of each day.

- Prioritize every item on your to-do list.

Cluttered Desk:

- Realize that a cluttered desk is postponed decisions.

- Clear your desk.

- Work on one task at a time to help yourself concentrate and think clearly.

- Have only the work you are currently doing on your desk, keeping other items somewhere else.

Long Lunch Hours:

- Realize that time is money and that lost time is never found again.

Personal Disorganization:

- Schedule and prioritize everything you do.

- Realize that time is money and that lost time is never found again.

Travel and Driving Time:

- Listen to motivational or educational audiotapes while you travel.

- Always have something to do while you travel.

- Remember that you do have some choice about where you live.

- Send someone else.

- Make sure you can't accomplish your purpose with a fax, letter, e-mail, phone call, or conference call before you set out.

- If possible, postpone a trip until you will be in the area anyway by suggesting, "I'll be in your area in three weeks. Can it wait until then?"

Ineffective Delegation:

- Train your team members to do tasks that don't require your expertise.

- Don't permit "upward" delegation.

- Never take on a problem from someone who reports to you unless he or she has suggested a solution.

Daydreaming:

- Realize that time is your most priceless resource.

- Ask yourself whether daydreaming is going to help you accomplish any of your goals.

Attempting Too Much:

- Focus on what's really important.

- Don't work compulsively on unimportant tasks.

- Prioritize everything you do, then work on "A" priorities before "B"s, and so on.

- Be realistic about what you can really do.

Working Smarter by Using Time Management Techniques

Excessive Socializing:

• Realize that time is money and that lost time is never found again.

• Remember that scheduling time for friends and leisure is important.

Unrealistic Time Estimates:

• Keep track of what you do in 15-minute time intervals for one week to get a better feel for how long things take.

Failure to Perform Tasks Correctly:

• Visualize yourself as a winner.

• Remember that successful people rarely make the same mistake twice.

• Have a back-up plan for when things go wrong.

Confused Responsibility:

• Be sure that you're clear about what's expected of you when your manager delegates something to you.

• Summarize often.

Lack of Clear Communication:

• Be sure that you're clear about what's expected of you when your manager delegates something to you.

• Summarize often.

• Make an extra effort to ensure that other people involved also understand what's expected.

Watching Television:

• Mark the programs you want to watch in the television schedule at the beginning of the week, then watch only those programs.

- Turn the television off as soon as the program is over, leaving the room to do something on your to-do list.

- Use your videocassette recorder to record the programs you want to watch, play them back at a convenient time, and fast forward through the commercials.

Surfing the Web:

- Put practical limits, such as one or two hours a week, on your Web-surfing time.

- Schedule your Web-surfing time in your datebook organizer.

- Resist the temptation to waste time on the Web, asking yourself whether what you're doing will put you closer to one of your high-priority goals.

Failure to Have a Place for Things:

- List the things you often have trouble finding.

- Write down where you plan to keep those items in the future and always put them in the places you have identified.

Procrastination:

- Clear the clutter.

- Establish an environment that's conducive to getting the job done.

- Use to-do lists effectively.

- Divide and conquer.

- Picture the end result of the finished job.

- Keep a record of what tasks you procrastinated on, why, and how you can minimize the problem next time.

Disorganized Spouse:

• Share this book with your spouse and show him or her how it has helped you.

• Obtain a videotape on time management from the library or one of the sources listed in Chapter Ten, watch it together, and discuss how your spouse can use the information to get better organized.

Now that you've identified your top five time-wasters and learned ways to combat them, make a commitment to yourself. Use the sheet on the following pages to list your time-wasters and how you plan to eliminate them from your life.

In the next chapter, you'll learn how to control stress. Since most people have never had any stress-management training, this may be the most important chapter for you.

My Top Five Time-Wasters

Time-Waster _____

To minimize this time-waster I will:

1.

2.

3.

4.

5.

Time-Waster _____

To minimize this time-waster I will:

1.

2.

3.

4.

5.

Working Smarter by Using Time Management Techniques

Time-Waster _____

To minimize this time-waster I will:

1.

2.

3.

4.

5.

Time-Waster _____

To minimize this time-waster I will:

1.

2.

3.

4.

5.

Time-Waster _____

To minimize this time-waster I will:

1.

2.

3.

4.

5.

• *Chapter Seven* •

Controlling Stress

Worry is the misuse of imagination.
　　　　　—Author Unknown

Stress now tops the list of causes of physical and emotional illnesses among U.S. workers. In fact, the National Council on Compensation reports that workplace stress is behind more than 13 percent of all occupational disease claims. About three-quarters of North Americans say that their job causes stress in their lives, an amount of stress that costs businesses up to $150 billion a year. A survey by a large life insurance company found that 34 percent of respondents had considered quitting because of stress, and that 14 percent had already done so.

If you have too much stress in your life, you will get sick. If you are sick, you can't practice good time management. If you don't practice good time management, you won't be able to achieve your goals. Stress is a necessary part of life, however. The secret to success is to control the bad stress in your life.

My favorite two definitions of stress are these:

1. Stress is any threat that requires us to adapt.

2. Stress is a biochemical response to a perceived threat.

The way you react to stress affects both your short-term and long-term health. The important word is "react." It's not the stress itself but how your body and mind respond to the stress that makes the difference in stress' impact on your life.

Fight or Flight

Every time you face a stressful situation, you experience what is called a "fight or flight" or "hit, run, or hide" response. Nature designed this biochemical mechanism to help humans confront or escape threats to their survival. The response has helped humanity survive by providing the extra strength and quick thinking needed to overcome threats. In today's world, threats in your physical environment aren't the only things that trigger this response. Thoughts and feelings elicit this response, too. Your brain does not discriminate among stressors.

Physical Reactions

When you perceive a threat either real or imagined, your body starts reacting. Here are some of the physical manifestations of the fight or flight response:

• Pupils dilate to let in more light

• Pulse rate increases

• Blood pressure increases

• Digestion slows to divert blood to the brain and muscles

• Coagulating ability increases

• Hormones, such as adrenaline and cortisol, are released from the endocrine glands

• Breathing rate increases

• Immune system is inhibited

Stress Symptoms

There are three basic types of stress symptoms:

1. Psychological or emotional symptoms, such as depression, overeating, lack of interest in sex, anger toward supervisors and co-workers, and crying at work

2. Physical symptoms, such as fatigue, headache, backache, insomnia, anxiety, palpitations, stomach problems, skin problems, and colds and flu

3. Job performance symptoms, such as making mistakes, feeling disorganized, and having trouble concentrating

Work and Stress

The type of work you do can affect your general stress level. Many jobs are considered high-stress jobs. Your organizational rank can also influence your stress level. One of the biggest stressors is change.

Stress is a normal response. If you don't control it, the results can range from annoying nervousness or worry to disabling headaches, nausea, indigestion, muscle pain, panic attacks, or chest pain. If you control stress and channel it correctly, however, it can actually help you. It can make you more alert, give you more energy, and help you work better than you normally do.

Stress Management

When something goes wrong, people tend to pile more problems on top of the first. Like a log-jam in a river, the result is to raise stress levels to painful new heights. Here are some effective ways of dealing with stress:

• Eliminate or reduce the cause of stress.

• Change your perception of the cause of stress and change your reaction to it.

• Avoid burnout by scheduling an hour a day for yourself and spending it doing something that is personally rewarding. The result will be better performance during work hours.

Using Your Brain to Reduce Stress

Try relieving stress by identifying which brain hemisphere you're using and then using the other hemisphere for a while. If time management issues are making you feel stressed, for example, you are overworking your left hemisphere. Switch to your right hemisphere and get in touch with your creative and emotional side by singing or listening to your favorite music. If you feel depressed or emotionally drained, your stress is located in the right hemisphere. Switch to the left hemisphere by organizing papers or doing math.

Foods and Stress

Food can't reduce stress. But eating certain foods during times of stress can help you stay healthy enough to deal with your stress. Of course, you should consult with your physician before changing your diet. And you should exercise moderation when it comes to portion size. With those caveats in mind, here are some suggestions for adults under stress:

- Drink eight to 10 eight-ounce glasses of water a day. Most of us don't drink enough water, which is good for you and can increase your energy level over several weeks.

- Consume dairy products to make sure you get enough calcium and protein. You should drink two one-cup portions of nonfat milk a day.

- Eat four to six four-ounce portions of fresh fruits and vegetables a day to get the recommended amount of vitamin C and potassium.

- Eat two three-ounce portions of fish, poultry, and low-fat meat a day to give your body the protein, B vitamins, iron, calcium, and vitamin A it needs.

- Eat several four-ounce portions of starches and cereals to ensure adequate fiber and vitamins.

Eating the wrong foods can compound the effects of stress by weakening you or further stimulating an already overstimulated nervous system. Food and beverages to avoid while under stress include:

- Caffeine, a stimulant and diuretic that stimulates the nervous system and makes some people irritable and jittery

- Alcohol, a depressant and diuretic that interferes with the absorption of B vitamins

- Large quantities of simple carbohydrates, which increase serotonin and may cause sleepiness and decreased efficiency

- Salt, which increases water retention and may make you look and feel worse

Twenty Five Stress-Reduction Tips

There are many ways to reduce stress. Try some of these suggestions:

1. Mild exercise can reduce stress. Even a casual walk can reduce stress. Go outside and escape from familiar surroundings if only for a few minutes. The fresh air will invigorate you. Note: If you have any health problems, are pregnant, or are over 40, consult your physician before beginning mild exercise.

2. Vigorous exercise, such as swimming, cycling, running, skiing, tennis, skating, surfing, basketball, or aerobics, can encourage your body to release endorphins, increase your heart rate, increase your blood circulation, strengthen your muscles, and calm your nerves. Note: If you have any health problems, are pregnant, or are over 40, consult your physician before beginning vigorous exercise.

3. Breathe deeply. Taking three deep breaths can make you feel tranquil.

4. Talk to a trusted friend who will listen without judging. Therapists are also trained to help you find solutions. Talking out problems can give you a fresh perspective and help you find solutions you might have overlooked.

5. Meditation and yoga can help calm you through silence and relaxed breathing. When you get angry and tense, you often forget to breathe. Appropriate breathing and time away from stressors will release your anxiety and add years to your life.

6. Laugh. Put humor into your life every day. It takes 15 facial muscles to smile and 43 to frown, which means that it's easier to smile than to frown. Laugh—out loud and often. When you're laughing, your body can't stay tense.

7. Listen to jazz, easy-listening music, and classical music, which can soothe your nerves and put your problems in perspective.

8. Take a nap. Research has proven that most arguments occur when people are tired. When you feel yourself getting angry, ask yourself, "Am I rested enough to tackle this problem, or do I need a little nap to rejuvenate myself first?" When you're rested, your stress level goes down.

9. Read about issues that concern you. No problems are new. Somebody somewhere has already experienced what you're going through. Reading about them will give you hope and give you a new perspective on your situation.

10. Brainstorm your way to solutions. Keep asking yourself, "What are my other options?"

11. Limit your caffeine intake. Coffee, tea, and cola stimulate your nervous system and initiate the process of stress arousal.

12. Limit your salt intake. Chips, fast food, and other salty foods may increase your blood pressure and your stress arousal.

13. Cut back on sugar. For many people, candy, cookies, cake, and doughnuts are favorite snacks thanks to the quick energy boost they provide. A short while later, however, the sugar blues set in. The result is often increased tiredness and irritability.

14. Eliminate most of the alcohol from your life. Although alcohol produces a deceptive feeling of peace, anything beyond a glass of wine at dinner leads to poorer concentration and increased stress.

15. Try a massage. Massage can relax tense muscles.

16. Take a hot shower or bath. Heat relaxes your muscles. You'll probably feel better almost immediately.

17. Don't sweat the small stuff. Ask yourself how important your problem will seem 10 years from now. If the answer is "not very," try to see beyond the problem and move on. Walk away from stress when possible. Setting a new goal may be what you need.

18. Declare a truce in family battles.

19. Visualize yourself achieving new goals.

20. Eliminate negative chatter from your life.

21. List all the things you enjoy doing and schedule time for them. Do something you enjoy at least three times a week, even if it's only for an hour at a time.

22. Set priorities and organize your time accordingly.

23. Learn to say no when someone asks you to do something stressful, if that's appropriate. Of course, you can't use this tip in every situation or you'll just create more problems for yourself.

24. List the stressful situations in your life and divide them into things you can't control or avoid and things you can. Focus your energy on the things you can control. Trying to conquer everything else is just a waste of energy.

25. Use your time and talents effectively. Working smarter will increase your productivity and your self-esteem, which may be just the boost you need.

If none of these tips works, seek professional assistance. And remember that the skills you acquire by reading this book will help you reduce stress by increasing your confidence and coping skills.

In the next chapter, you'll learn how to get better at what you do every day.

• *Chapter Eight* •

Getting Better at What You Do Every Day

Every job is a self-portrait of the person who did it. Autograph your work with excellence.

—Author Unknown

Spending an hour a day for six months on a new topic can make you very knowledgeable about something you know nothing about today. That's 180 hours of study. Whether you learn by reading, listening to audiotapes, watching videotapes, undertaking self-study programs, attending seminars and workshops, or talking to experts, every hour counts.

Managers and leaders need numerous skills to achieve success. This chapter focuses on three of them:

• Giving better presentations

• Building teams and creating a motivational climate for your staff

• Maintaining a positive mental attitude

What skills are you going to work on? Every day you should work to get a little better at what you do.

Giving Better Presentations

One of the challenges managers and leaders face is learning how to communicate better. Whether it's an in-house continuing education seminar, a presentation to a client, or a request for additional help at peak periods, there are ways to make presentations more effective. The following 15 points will help you communicate better, earn higher ratings from your audience, and achieve better outcomes.

1. Make sure that your presentation covers what the title, abstract or program description says it's going to cover. Don't give a different talk! Your audience decided to attend your talk based on the abstract or program description.

2. Give your audience state-of-the-art information about how to do something. "How to" programs usually earn the highest ratings and attract the best attendance.

3. Concentrate on ideas, not data. When it comes to holding an audience's attention, ideas are far more effective than facts and figures. Your audience doesn't care about all the data you labored to obtain. People want to know what your figures mean, why they're important, and what they need to do in response. Instead of reciting facts and figures to convince your audience, present your ideas logically and then select a few facts and figures to back them up.

4. Don't turn your back on your audience while you're speaking.

5. Use hand-outs instead of slides whenever possible. The best and highest paid speakers these days use very few slides. That's because most audiences don't care about them. What they want are more and better hand-outs to take with them after a presentation. Limit your use of overhead projectors to audiences of fewer than 25 people.

6. Don't hide behind your slides if you use them. Most of us were taught to speak to our slides. Don't do it. Instead, speak to your audience. Use a laser pointer to draw attention to points of interest. And don't ever say, "I know you can't read this slide." Slides the audience can't read are both a waste of time and an insult to the audience. As a result, they'll lose respect for you. Before you show slides, check them out in a room the same size you will be speaking in. If you can't read the slide from the back of the room, don't use it. During your actual presentation, keep the lights as bright as possible but not so bright the slides can't be seen.

7. Don't stand behind a lectern the entire time. Stand away from the lectern, returning to it only to refer to your notes.

8. Use a public address system for groups of more than 20 people. If you move away from the lectern, you'll need a wireless microphone or a clip-on microphone with 25 feet of cord that is not taped down. Request wireless or clip-on microphones in advance and test the system at least an hour before the program starts to make sure it's working correctly.

9. Start on time and end on time or even early. Whatever you do, don't go over your allotted time.

10. Remember that the mind can take only as much as the seat can stand! Allowing a 15-minute break every hour and a half to two hours is a good rule of thumb.

11. Audiotape your presentation and listen to it later as a way of improving future presentations. Remember, unless your tape recorder batteries are weak the way you sound on tape is the way you sound to others. Try to eliminate "dead time" from your presentation.

12. Make sure everyone can hear everything. Speak to the people in the back of the room. Don't mumble. If a member of the audience asks a question, restate it so that everyone knows what you're responding to.

13. Avoid ethnic, religious, or political jokes. Although you may get some laughs, some people will be offended. But don't be afraid to use jokes, magic, sight gags, and other forms of humor to keep your audience's attention. Practice them to ensure that they're effective. And remember that humor is a serious business!

Great Teachers

Presentations can be great teaching tools. Effective teachers share the following characteristics:

• They are constantly learning more about their subject.

• They are excited and passionate about the material they're presenting.

- They look for implications by regularly reviewing materials both related and unrelated to their subject.

- They are centered on their subject and their audience.

- They control program flow but build flexibility into the program.

- They are flexible and can adapt without complaint to any physical environment.

Team Building

One of the challenges that managers and leaders face is hiring and retaining quality staff members. Team-building will be even more important in the 21st century. The better your team performs, the better you will look and be. Teamwork leads to extraordinary performance. People who underperform as individuals often give peak performance when brought together as teams. A team can manage big jobs better than an individual. Managing teams requires different skills than managing individuals, however. The key to motivating teams is involvement!

Many people don't want to work on teams. They like to work alone. They don't want to change. Try some of the suggestions in Chapter Four to convince your employees to try the team approach.

Retaining Employees

Employees leave for a variety of reasons. Some of the major causes include the following:

- Twenty-eight percent join a competing firm.

- Twenty-eight percent change professions.

- Twelve percent leave to attend school.

- Nine percent work for vendors.

- Five percent retire.

The remainder leave for other reasons.

People don't usually change jobs just for money unless they can earn significantly more at a new job. Most people change jobs because they're searching for new opportunities or responding to how they've been treated at their old jobs.

Here are some tips for retaining employees:

- Provide skill-development programs and let employees know they are being prepared for new challenges.

- Provide a climate that people want to work in.

- Encourage positive, personal relationships among employees.

- Don't assume that people who have been top achievers in line positions will be effective leaders. A great bench medical technologist, for example, won't necessarily be a great laboratory manager. Management and leadership skills are different from the hands-on skills that line workers use to solve problems. Provide new managers with training to develop their leadership skills. Good managers are made, not born. Leadership is a profession!

- Let people know how important they are to the organization.

- Give people frequent opportunities to be proud of themselves.

- Delegate as much authority as possible.

- Give people credit and recognition when they deserve it.

- Make jobs as challenging, interesting, and varied as possible.

Motivation

Can you get people excited? Are your people willing to go the extra mile for you? Here are some tips for working with team members:

1. Let team members know what you expect from them. Don't assume that they know. Tell them!

2. Keep team members informed. Everyone likes to know what's happening.

3. Give team members control. People respond in astounding ways when they are given even a little control over the work they do.

4. Give team members start-to-finish responsibility. Don't fragment responsibilities. Doing little pieces of work doesn't turn people on!

5. Make team members champions. Make them feel good about themselves by showing that you believe their work is important, that you're excited about it, and that you are confident they'll do a great job.

6. Give team members feedback. People want to know how they're doing.

7. Reward team members. And remember that money isn't the only reward. Try using personal congratulations, verbal recognition, personal notes, increased responsibility, or performance-based promotions.

8. Help team members learn and grow. You are the catalyst that will encourage people to develop themselves. Create a positive environment for your staff. Encourage everyone to share information and solutions by sharing information and solutions yourself.

9. Stay approachable. Ensure that people are comfortable coming to you with problems.

Team Building

Here are some team building tips:

• Make sure that your organization's mission, philosophy, and goals are written down and that everyone understands them. Explain administrative and managerial goals.

• Hire people smarter than you.

• Evaluate employees' results, not their activities.

- Promote from within whenever possible. You'll attract and keep the best employees if they see opportunities.

- Listen and respond to employees' complaints.

- The best way to determine how to motivate people? Ask them!

- Manage by example.

- Manage by wandering around. Be visible in the workplace!

- If you're not innovating, you're decaying.

- Praise in public; discipline in private. Treat employees with respect.

- Criticize ideas, not the people who come up with them.

- Remember the four to one rule: Every time you criticize a worker's performance, give him or her four compliments.

- All people act out of self-interest. Link individual and organizational goals.

- Manage as though you had no authority. Lead by the quality of your ideas.

- Seek understanding when you communicate, not agreement.

- Ask employees to bring possible solutions to you when they bring problems.

- Make change your organization's norm.

- Have an active style, not a reactive one.

- Greet people by name.

- Look people in the eye when you talk to them.

- Build your team's independence and interdependence.

- Be sure every job description includes performance standards.

- Build people's self-esteem. The more competent people feel, the more they're able to contribute.

- Don't promote people who have only earned a salary increase.

- Allow intelligent mistakes.

- Build on your people's strengths instead of focusing on their weaknesses.

- The first sign of decay is the inability to attract and challenge competent people.

- Keep your business a good place to work.

- Docking pay or issuing official reprimands to employees who are frequently late, show decreased productivity, or have other problems often results in resentment rather than positive results. Using appraisal sessions and reward systems to create incentives for improvement is a better idea.

- Postponing or ignoring employee performance reviews can be counterproductive. Approximately 45 percent of workers don't know where they stand with their bosses. That lowers morale and decreases productivity. Delays also deny managers the opportunity to tell staff members how they can improve their work. Plus, a review can protect the company against dismissal suits. Those who have been warned are far less likely to sue.

- When employees feel they are being treated fairly, their performance improves. In one poll, businesses that scored high on fairness measures had fewer employee absences and injuries.

- Managers greatly increase workers' commitment to the organization when they listen carefully to employees' suggestions and take them seriously. Listen actively!

- Performance generally increases during a worker's first five years on the job, then levels off unless the worker receives a new challenge.

Longevity incentives, which encourage the worker to stay with the business, make the most sense during the first five years. After that, a performance-based incentive plan makes more sense.

• Follow through on agreements.

• Help people grow in their jobs.

• Build bridges, not walls.

• Extend the benefit of the doubt.

• Create a workplace where people think their strengths are more important than their weaknesses.

• Constant negative messages can actually inhibit performance. Instead of being confrontational, think of yourself as a coach.

A Positive Mental Attitude

Zig Ziglar once said, "I've never met an enthusiastic failure." He also said, "It's your attitude, not your aptitude, that determines your altitude."

You can work hard and smart, but if you don't have a positive mental attitude you are destroying your chances of success. Being positive is essential to success. Being positive is a discipline, and you can control your moods. A mood simply reflects your attitude. You can change both. You can program yourself to be positive. And the more adversity you face, the more positive you have to be.

Negativity is polluting the atmosphere. Whether it's family members, co-workers, or a cynical culture, we are surrounded by naysayers and negative people. Negative people are usually the worst role models, because they look for reasons things won't work. As a result, they're more prone to failure. What should you do about all the negativity that surrounds you? Although there's no way to get rid of it, you must block it out. The simplest way is to let negative people know face-to-face that their behavior is bothering you and that they could really help by acting more positively. If this fails, give the negative person a book, magazine article, audiotape, or videotape that might help them take a more positive approach to things. Or you could ask someone this person likes to talk to him or her about the importance of a positive attitude. You can only do so much!

Eliminate these three words from your vocabulary: never, can't, and unreachable.

Having a positive attitude means giving 100 percent when less would suffice. You have a choice about what attitude you adopt. If you feel angry, it's because you've chosen to feel that way. If you feel happy, it's because you've chosen to feel that way. A positive attitude won't help you do anything, but it will help you do everything better than a negative attitude! If you are a positive person, you can get a lot more done through other people.

Do you know that old saying, "You can't control the wind, but you can adjust your sails"? That's what a winning attitude does for you. It helps you recognize unavoidable circumstances and adjust your sails so you can move forward. It helps you maneuver beyond temporary defeat and makes you unconquerable.

People listen to the radio station WIIFM, which stands for "What's in it for Me." They also listen to station MMFI, which stands for "Make Me Feel Important." People who feel good about themselves feel good about their work. Personal power is a combination of a positive attitude, enthusiasm, energy, and optimism.

The following qualities express positive attitudes:

• Honesty

• Agreeability

• Willingness to listen

• Dependability

• Loyalty

• Enthusiasm

• Confidence

• Responsibility

• Cooperativeness

- Open-mindedness

- Decisiveness

- Integrity

- Willingness to work hard

- Friendliness

- Generosity

- Trustworthiness

- Persistence

- Dedication

- Ability to learn

- Energy

You can use a technique called self-talk to instill these qualities in yourself. Based on behavioral research, self-talk is a way of programming your brain as if it were a computer. Just as a software program gives new information to a computer, self-talk provides new software for your brain. It reprograms your mind, and your behavior changes as a result of the new messages your brain is receiving. Remember, you have a choice about most of what you hear. Avoid negative self-talk. Allow only positive self-talk.

Reactions

How do you react to stressful situations? See which column best describes your reactions to stress:

Negative Reaction	*Positive Reaction*
Making insulting remarks	Talking things over
Overeating	Physical exercise

Irritability	Relaxation exercises
Headaches	Deep breathing
Controlling	Letting others participate
Tight neck and shoulders	Stretching exercises
Rushing, worrying, becoming angry	Organizing, prioritizing
Overspending	Budgeting
Feeling fearful	Asking for help
Negative thoughts	Positive self-talk
Blaming others	Accepting responsibility
Yelling, hitting	Counseling

Negative thinkers make things hard on themselves and others. When was the last time you felt enthusiastic about working with a negative person? Probably never! Consider the attitudes of the people in the following example:

Bob Robert	**Mary Beth**
It's all screwed up. We really blew it.	Let's not make the same mistake again. How can we keep this from happening again? What can we learn from this mistake?
Laboratory X really beat us bad. They got all the work from the new health maintenance organization.	We're much better than they are. Let's set a goal and plan to get the work back.
This is a terrible idea. It will never work.	Let's brainstorm and see what we can come up with.

Things are getting worse around here.	We can make things better. Let's figure out a way to make improvements.

Are you more like Bob Robert or Mary Beth? Who would you rather have on your team? Who makes the best impression? Chances are that you aren't as positive as you could be. Try recording yourself in conversations and meetings. You'll probably discover that you're sometimes more like Bob Robert than Mary Beth, even though you think of yourself as a positive thinker.

A negative mental attitude will hurt your career. A positive mental attitude will help. Of course, having a positive attitude doesn't mean that you simply accept everything that comes along with a big smile. It does mean that you look at every situation and choose the best reaction strategy. It takes effort, discipline, practice, and work to have a positive mental attitude. You can't change your entire approach to life overnight. All of us are conditioned to find things wrong and to focus on the negative. Keep telling yourself, "Just for today, I'm going to postpone negative thinking and look on the positive side. I will concentrate on how to make things better rather than focus on the fact that they're broken. I'll keep my mind open to new ideas and solutions."

In the next chapter, we'll summarize what you have learned about overachieving in business and in life.

• *Chapter Nine* •

Overachieving in Business and Life

Learning is defined as a change in behavior. You haven't learned a thing until you can take action and use it.

—Don Shula and Ken Blanchard

The term "overachiever" is often associated with the workaholic who is never satisfied with excellence and is always trying to achieve perfection. Some people actually try to avoid overachievement. In reality, overachieving is a positive quality. Overachieving means making that extra effort; it's about working smart, being organized, having goals, and sticking to your plan until you reach those goals.

Being an overachiever requires that you change your habits and embrace the seven steps outlined in this book. A habit is a tendency to act in a certain way that is reinforced by repetition. A bad habit is any habit that doesn't serve you positively. Keeping bad habits keeps you from achieving excellence and success.

If you make a habit of doing the right things the right way, you will increase the odds that you will achieve success more consistently. Remember, practice makes perfect. Incorporating this book's seven steps into your life can help you start changing your habits. Don't try to do it all at once. Divide and conquer by breaking your goals into smaller units outlined in a plan. When you practice good habits, success becomes second nature.

This book's seven steps offer you a blueprint for overachievement. You have walked through the steps one at a time. Now let's remind ourselves how to begin the cycle of success by giving ourselves a management tune-up.

Step One: Put balance in your life with written goals.

People make their dreams into realities by working hard to achieve written goals. Do you know any retired person who wishes they had spent more time in the lab or at the office? Probably not! But we all know people who wish they had spend more time with their loved ones, a hobby, or a second career.

Goals are how you make your dreams come true. They are the individual steps you must take as you pursue those dreams. Make sure that your goals are clear and realistic. As you develop your plan for reaching your goals, remember to divide and conquer. Break your goals into smaller segments that are more easily achievable. Be sure to develop goals that balance the seven important areas of life: mental, physical, spiritual, social, financial, career, and family.

Step Two: Create a plan for reaching your goals — and stick to it.

Most of us have many more things to do than we can possibly accomplish each day. Successful people set priorities as they work toward their goals. Unsuccessful people perform random activities. You must decide what to do and what not to do. If you fail to plan, you automatically plan to fail. Planning is the key to success.

Remember the difference between efficiency and effectiveness. Efficiency means doing the job right and effectiveness means doing the right job efficiently. Don't work on the wrong thing! Developing goals and prioritizing them gives you a rudder that allows you to steer your ship in the right direction. Without that rudder, your ship would simply go whatever direction the wind blows. In the business world, a rudderless ship means you spend your time managing crises. Adopt the philosophy that lack of proper planning on someone else's part does not create an emergency on your part.

Step Three: Expect the unexpected and become a master of change.

Are you a change master? Are you ready for new opportunity? The secret of success in life is to be ready for opportunity when it comes. Don't let what you can't do interfere with what you can do. Gary Player said, "The harder I work, the luckier I get." That's because luck is opportunity meeting preparation. When you're through changing, you're through. Master the skills you need to move you to the next level. View change as something positive, because change always leads to new opportunities.

Step Four: Learn from past mistakes and successes.

Learning what not to do is just as important as learning what to do. Overachievers don't have a magic formula. They are overachievers because they set exciting goals, use their creativity, and don't let problems overwhelm them. They never give up. In fact, they see problems as opportunities. You can, too.

On the road to success, you don't just learn from your own experiences. You need to have role models and mentors. You can learn a lot from other people's mistakes and successes. They can tell us about pitfalls to avoid and show us the way. Use other people as resources, or you'll be shortchanging yourself.

Step Five: Work smarter by using time management techniques.

If you want to work smarter rather than harder, you need to use time management techniques. Effective time management requires a system, discipline, planning, and flexibility. When you practice effective time management, you boost your self-esteem. That in turn improves your productivity. Thus, effective time management can launch you into a positive cycle of improved productivity.

Step Six: Control stress.

Worry is the misuse of imagination. And the way you react to stress can affect your short-term and long-term health. The important word is "react." It's not stress itself but how your body and mind respond to it that makes the difference. If you respond badly, you'll get sick. If you're sick, you can't manage your time effectively. If you're not managing your time effectively, you can't achieve your goals. Don't let stress keep you from success. To deal with stress effectively, eliminate or reduce the stressors in your life, change the way you view stress, and learn to react more effectively. Exercise, deep breathing, and humor can help.

Step Seven: Get better at what you do every day.

If you spent an hour a day learning something new, in six months you could be extremely knowledgeable about something you know nothing about today. That's 180 hours of study. When was the last time you made that kind of commitment to learning something new? Every hour is important.

Learning how to give effective presentations, create a climate that motivates your team, and keep a positive mental attitude are skills you need to achieve success. Remember that there's a difference between striving for excellence and striving for perfection. Excellence is attainable, gratifying, and healthy. Perfection is often unattainable and frustrating.

The Secret of Success

Where can you find the secret of success? Look in the mirror. The secret is you! Only you can create your success, and only I can create mine. The 10 most powerful two-letter words in the English language are "If it is to be, it is up to me."

Staying successful once you achieve your goals demands that you constantly test new ideas, admit mistakes, and rapidly follow through on ideas that work. Good luck! I hope you make a difference.

Am I Making A Difference?
—Author Unknown

I saw them tearing a building down,
A gang of men in my hometown.
With a heave, and a ho, and a "Yes! Yes!" yell,
They swung a beam and a sidewall fell.
I said to the foreman, "Are these men skilled
As the ones you'd use if you had to build?"
He laughed and said, "Oh no! Indeed!
The most common labor is all I need!
Because I can destroy in a day or two
What it takes a builder 10 years to do!"
I thought to myself as I went my way,
Which of these roles am I willing to play?
Am I the one who is tearing down,
As I carelessly make my way around?
Or am I one who builds with care
So that my profession and my community,
Are just a little better, because I was there?

One of my favorite riddles is relevant to the topic of success. Three frogs were sitting on a lily pad. One decided to jump. How many frogs

92

were left on the lily pad? Think about it for a minute. The answer is three! Deciding to jump is a thought, but jumping is an action. Are you going to think about using what you've learned in this book or are you going to use it? The decision is yours.

In the final chapter, you'll find additional resources you can use as you undergo your self-management tune-up.

• *Chapter Ten* •

Additional Resources

If you read or listen to something often enough, no one can take it away from you.

—Author Unknown

Here are some additional resources you can use as you continue your quest for success. I have used all of the resources listed here and recommend them personally.

General

Alessandra, T., and O'Connor, M.J., *The Platinum Rule*. New York: Warner Books, Inc., 1996.

Living by the platinum rule means treating people how they want to be treated, not how you want to be treated. This excellent book is full of practical information about how to use the platinum rule. You'll also learn about the four basic personalities.

Drucker, P.F., *The Effective Executive*. New York: Harper & Row, 1967.

This book claims that effective executives have five "habits of mind." They know where their time goes, focus on outward contributions, build on their strengths and weaknesses, spend time in areas where superior performance will bring outstanding results, and do things in the right sequence.

Frings, C.S., "Rethinking Ourselves for Success in the 21st Century." *Clinical Laboratory News*, Volume 22: Number 1, January 1996.

My article discusses current and future changes in the health-care arena. You'll learn what tools you'll need to have in your toolbox if you want to be successful in the next century.

Frings, C.S., *Self-Management & Leadership Strategies for Succeeding in the 21st Century*. Birmingham: Chris Frings & Associates, 1995.

This audiotape reviews many of the concepts discussed in this book. Aimed at anyone who wants to become a better manager and leader, it is also a great way to give yourself or a colleague a self-management tune-up.

Frings, C.S., *Self-Management & Leadership Strategies for Succeeding in the 21st Century*. Birmingham: Chris Frings & Associates, 1996.

This hour-and-a-half-long videotape serves as a self-management and leadership tune-up, not a major overhaul. Highly entertaining, the videotape combines my best magic with my best public speaking. Both informational and motivational, it addresses the seven skills you need to succeed in the 21st century. It's a great way to learn about self-management or simply review the material presented in this book.

Pitino, R., *Success Is a Choice*. New York: Bantam Doubleday Dell Publishing Group, Inc., 1997.

If you follow the 10-step program outlined in this book, you'll achieve more success than you ever thought possible.

Vance, M., and Deacon, D., *Think Outside the Box*. Franklin Lakes, NJ: Carter Press, 1995.

This book uses a matrix to plot the nine things that are necessary for fostering greater creativity: people, place, product, involvement, information, inspiration, caring, cooperation, and creativity. You'll learn how to connect these nine components and make them a part of your company's culture. Of course, you'll also learn how to think outside the box!

Yeomans, W.N., *1000 Things You Never Learned in Business School*. New York: A Mentor Book, 1985.

This book provides a lot of practical information that can help you develop the self- management skills you need to reach your goals.

Goals

Givens, C.J., *SuperSelf: Doubling Your Personal Effectiveness.* New York: Simon & Schuster, 1993.

This book reveals the secret of taking control of your life and keeping others from controlling your time. The focus is on common sense success strategies.

Wilson, S.B., *Goal Setting.* New York: American Management Association, 1994.

This book will help you decide where you want to go and how to get there.

Ziglar, Z., *Goals: Setting and Achieving Them on Schedule.* Chicago: Nightingale-Conant Corp., 1986.

This videotape will tell you how to set and reach goals—and convince you to write down your goals. I highly recommended this videotape to viewers interested in using a winning attitude to achieve their goals.

Ziglar, Z., *Over the Top.* Nashville: Thomas Nelson Publishers, 1994.

Ziglar's latest book will persuade you to commit to being the best you can be. The book will convince you that if you recognize and continue to develop what you have, you may astonish everyone.

Change

Burrus, D., *Technotrends: How to Use Technology to Go Beyond the Competition.* New York: HarperCollins Publishers, Inc., 1993.

This book will show you how to use tomorrow's tools to redefine quality, ir
tion, and service. The author is one of the world's leading technology for
ers.

Celente, G., *Trends 2000*. New York: Warner Books, Inc., 1997.

Written by one of the better trend forecasters, this book will tell you how t
pare for the next century's changes—and how to profit from them.

Smith, H., *Rethinking America*. New York: Random House, 1995.

This book points the way to creative and effective new ways to think,
work, and succeed in the future and shows how American innovators are
just that.

Wilkinson, I., "The Instant Change Master." *Clinical Laboratory News*, V
20: Number 7, July 1994.

This article will help make you an instant "change master."

Learning From Other People's Successes

Covey, S.R., *The Seven Habits of Highly Effective People*. New York: Sir
Schuster, 1990.

This book presents a holistic, integrated, principle-centered approach for
ing personal and professional problems. It presents a step-by-step pathw
living with fairness, integrity, honesty, and human dignity—principles th
give you the security you need to adapt to change and the wisdom and po
take advantage of the opportunities that change creates.

Griessman, B.E., *The Achievement Factors: Candid Interviews With Some
Most Successful People of Our Time*. San Marcos, CA: Slawson Communica
Inc., 1990.

Presenting a collection of short biographies, this book describes factors that seem to contribute to high achievers' success and offers a unique program you can follow on your own path to success.

Noble, S.P., ed., *301 Great Management Ideas From America's Most Innovative Small Companies*. Boston, MA: Inc. Publishing, 1991.

This book presents management tips in bite-size pieces, with one idea per page.

Pritchett, P., *Mindshift: The Employee Handbook for Understanding the Changing World of Work*. Dallas, TX: Pritchett & Associates, Inc., 1996.

This book describes the factors driving today's high-velocity change, explains where that change is taking us, and describes how we need to reframe our thinking to fit these new realities. The book will help you develop the mindset you need for success in the 21st century.

Van Fleet, J.K., *The 22 Biggest Mistakes Managers Make and How to Correct Them*. West Nyack, NY: Parker Publishing Co., 1982.

The title of this useful, practical book says it all.

Time Management

Alexander, R., *Common Sense Time Management*. New York: American Management Association, 1992.

This practical book is full of tips, techniques, and common-sense advice for solving common time management problems.

Frings, C.S., *The Hitchhiker's Guide to Effective Time Management*. Washington, DC: AACC Press, 1997.

My latest book on time management is a condensed version of my seminars and workshops. Packed with practical suggestions, the book presents more than 200 time management ideas. You'll learn how to work smarter and how to set up a 30-day plan that will allow you to free up two hours a day.

Frings, C.S., *Increasing Productivity Through Effective Time Management*. Birmingham: C.S. Frings & Associates, 1996.

This audiotape gives you 14 practical steps for managing your time better and tells you how to manage your time-wasters. I share some of the goal-setting techniques I used to retire at age 47 from a 20-year career and start a new life. If you follow my suggestions, you should be able to free up two hours daily.

Frings, C.S., *Increasing Productivity Through Effective Time Management*. Birmingham: C.S. Frings & Associates, 1996.

This hour-long videotape lets you sit in on one of my time management programs. The messages, jokes, and magic are all there. Informative and entertaining, this videotape is a great tool for learning or reviewing.

Frings, C.S., *Increasing Productivity Through Effective Time Management*. Birmingham: C.S. Frings & Associates, 1997.

I use this seminar manual in my half-day and full-day time management seminars. A great resource for consultants, it covers topics like setting and reaching goals, becoming a winner, controlling time-wasters, eliminating procrastination, managing interruptions, delegating effectively, enhancing motivation, and much more. If you try the ideas presented in this book, you'll be able to free up two hours a day.

Griessman, B.E., *Time Tactics of Very Successful People*. New York: McGraw Hill, Inc., 1994.

This best-selling time management book contains many practical strategies you can use to work smarter and increase your personal productivity.

Mayer, J.J., *Time Management for Dummies.* Foster City, CA: IDG Books, 1995.

This book provides a good, short course in time management. Very useful, it contains many practical ideas.

Winston, S., *The Organized Executive: New Ways to Manage Time, Paper, People & the Electronic Office.* New York: W.W. Norton & Co., Inc., 1994.

A must read for the serious time management student. Highly recommended.

Stress Management

Charlesworth, E., and Nathan, R.G., *Stress Management: A Comprehensive Guide to Wellness.* New York: Ballantine Books, 1984.

This excellent book contains a lot of useful information. I highly recommend it.

Gatto, R.P., *Controlling Stress in the Workplace.* San Diego, CA: Pfeiffer & Co., 1993.

This book will teach you how to manage stress that seems unmanageable.

Presentation Skills

Kushner, M., *Successful Presentations for Dummies.* Foster City, IL: IDG Books, 1996.

Packed with very practical information, this book is a great resource.

Peoples, D.A., *Presentations Plus,* 2nd ed. New York: John Wiley & Sons, Inc., 1992.

No matter what type of presentation you have to give, this book can help. It's packed with useful strategies, principles, and guidelines that will help you persuade your listeners.

Wilder, C., *The Presentations Kit: 10 Steps for Selling Your Ideas*. New York: John Wiley & Sons, Inc., 1990.

This book will teach you how to customize a presentation for maximum impact. Whether you have to deliver a report to management, sell an idea to prospective clients, or conduct a training seminar, this book will help you present information and persuade listeners.

Yarnell, M., and McCommon, K.B., *Power Speaking*. Evanston, IL: UCA Books, 1987.

This book will help you learn to communicate better by speaking more effectively.

Team Building

Bryant, P.B., and Geier, K.G., *Nothin' But a Winner*. Minneapolis: Sports Films & Talents, Inc., 1982.

In this 30-minute videotape, you will learn the secrets of successful football coach Paul "Bear" Bryant. These secrets can help you become a winner, too. You will learn this great manager's techniques for delegating, team-building, time management, planning, leadership, trust-building, and much, much more.

Frings, C.S., "Set a Climate for Motivation of Your Staff," *POL Observer*, Medical Economics, Volume 3, September/October 1995.

This article will teach you how to create a climate for motivating your team members.

Option Technologies, Inc., *Just-in-Time Knowledge for Teams: A Pocket Guide to Effective Team Performance*. Mendota Heights, MN: Option Technologies, Inc., 1992.

This publication contains a lot of practical information in a concise format.

Positive Mental Attitude

Canfield, J., and Hansen, M.V., *Chicken Soup for the Soul: 101 Stories to Open the Heart and Rekindle the Spirit.* Deerfield Beach, FL: Health Communications, Inc., 1993.

Whether you want to teach or inspire, you'll find just the right story in this heartwarming treasury. Check it out.

Chapman, E.N., *Attitude: Your Most Priceless Possession,* 2nd Edition. Menlo Park, CA: Crisp Publications, Inc., 1990.

This book will tell you everything you ever wanted to know about keeping a positive attitude.

Jones, C. *Tremendous, Life Is Tremendous.* Mechanicsburg, PA: Life Management Services, Inc., 1968.

This great motivational book discusses seven laws of leadership and describes ways of applying them to your life.

Paulson, T.L., *Making Humor Work: Take Your Job Seriously and Yourself Lightly.* Menlo Park, CA: Crisp Publications, 1989.

This book will introduce you to the value of humor on the job. You'll learn how to use humor to disarm anger, unlock people's receptivity, and enhance communication. See for yourself why it's never a crime to have fun on the job.